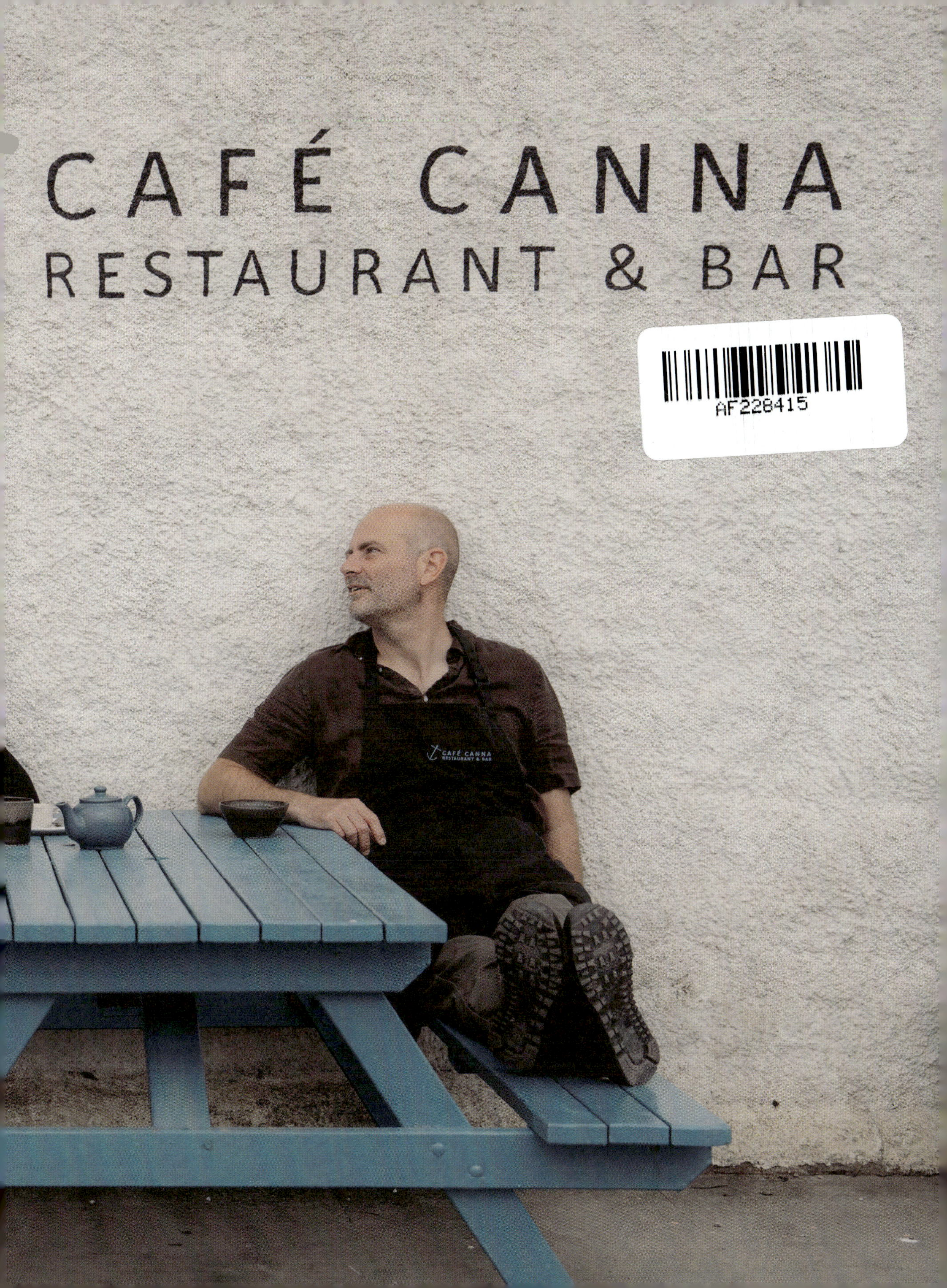
CAFÉ CANNA
RESTAURANT & BAR
CAFÉ CANNA
RESTAURANT & BAR

CAFÉ CANNA

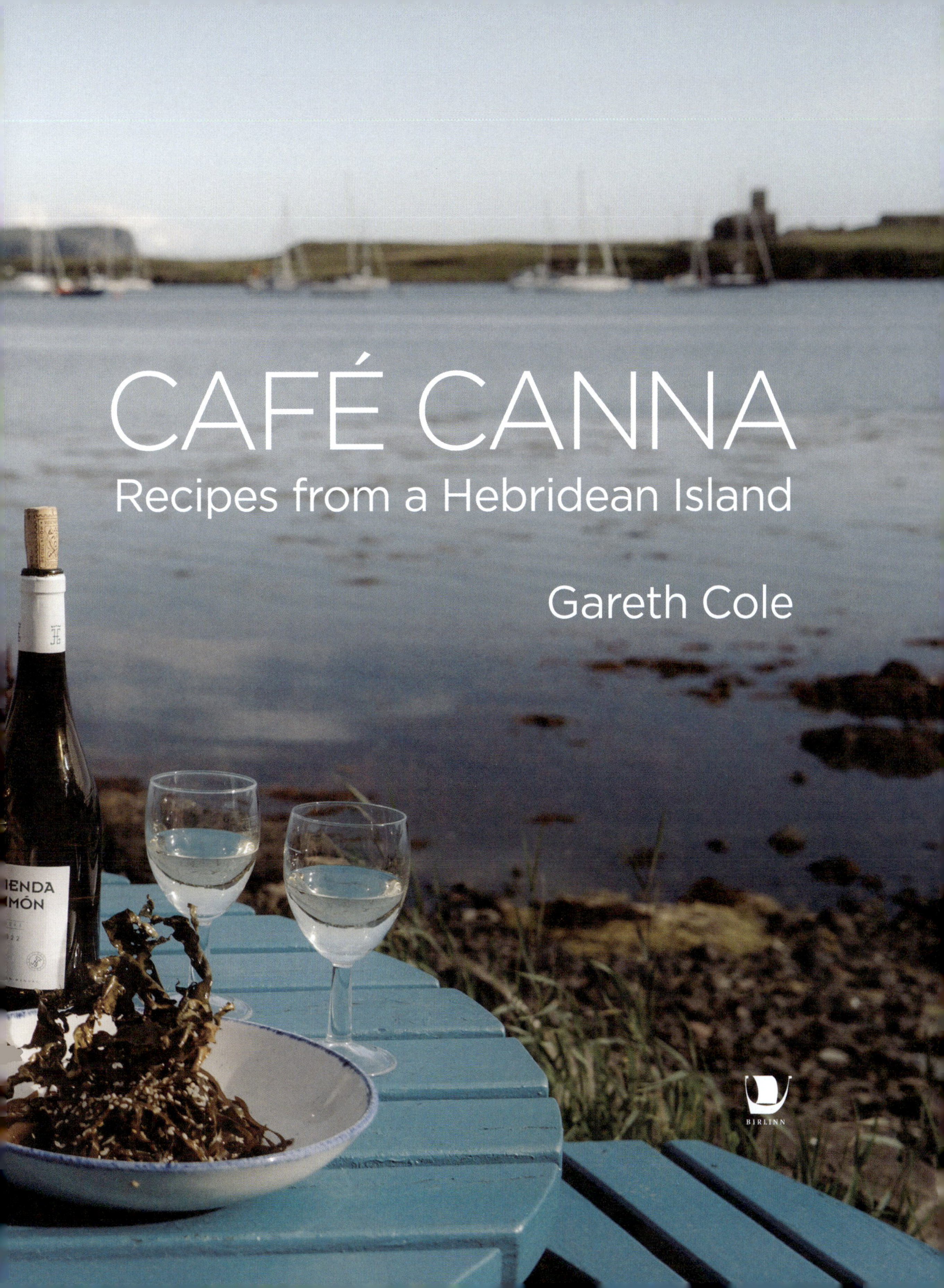

CAFÉ CANNA

Recipes from a Hebridean Island

Gareth Cole

This book is dedicated to Lesley Graham, without whom it – and many other books – would not have come about. With love and appreciation.

Hugh Andrew, Publisher

First published in 2024 by
Birlinn Limited
West Newington House
10 Newington Road
Edinburgh EH9 1QS

www.birlinn.co.uk

Text copyright © Gareth Cole 2024

Photography by Simon Hird (simonhird.com)
and Gareth Cole.

The moral right of Gareth Cole to be identified as the author of this work has been asserted by him in accordance with the Copyright, Designs and Patents Act 1988.

All rights reserved. No part of this publication may be reproduced, stored or transmitted in any form without the express written permission of the publisher.

ISBN: 978 1 78027 851 3

British Library Cataloguing-in-Publication Data
A catalogue record for this book is available from the British Library

Typeset by Mark Blackadder

Printed and bound by PNB, Latvia

To the Café Canna crew, past and present. Working a season here is not for the faint-hearted, and I count my lucky stars that every one of you has put so much into keeping this little raft on the rocking seas riding those waves. Every year sees a monumental effort and a ridiculous laugh. To anybody who has been staff – and any of you who have innocently thought you were visiting for a holiday and spent it on the dishwasher – thank you so very much.

Laurel – the one with the laugh that sounds like she's hyperventilating – deserves particular appreciation. The positive effect you've had on the place over the years is unstateable.

Most of all, to Indi and the latest recruit and world's most destructive kitchen hand, Hector, who's life in summer revolves in and around the restaurant, all the love and thanks I've got to give.

Contents

Welcome

Perched on a Hebridean island measuring two miles across and populated by eighteen residents, Café Canna is one of the remotest restaurants in the UK. By necessity (and no small measure of love), we make the most of island ingredients. Seaweed, which we forage from our shores, is one of our favourites. We land seafood from our crystal waters just moments before it is served. Meat comes from the surrounding lands and vegetables from our plot. We make our own bread every day. We even brew our own beer.

Running a restaurant in such a place has a certain inherent calamity. Secretly I think we like it that way. We're never quite sure what supplies the boat will deliver – and at best this is once or twice weekly. We've had to do without basic stock many times (try explaining that when the bar has run dry – hence starting the brewery). If something breaks, we (try to) fix it, and if the power goes down we cook by candlelight until we can sort it. This fragility has become a blessing – it has pushed us to be ever more self-reliant, and so ever more interested in the fabulous produce that can be sourced fresh and direct from our very own island.

Our confidence in making use of these ingredients has grown over the years and we have become a popular port of call for travellers of the islands. (It has to be said that visitors to Canna have little choice – we are the only eatery.)

This book is born out of the interest that people have shown for what we are trying to do – their tableside questions about where our ingredients come from, how to forage from the land and the seashore (I'm often asked about the seaweed, how to spot it, harvest it and make something delicious with it) – and the enthusiasm of our customers for sampling something different.

Gareth – chef, forager,
owner, brewer·

EVERYBODY IS INVOLVED

I'm originally from a little village in Deeside, Aberdeenshire, but I've been on Canna for a good while now. Long enough to say 'aye' on the inward rather than outward breath and to consider wellies desirable evening attire.

I didn't plan on coming to Canna specifically when I decided I wanted to live somewhere more remote, preferably on the west coast – I love sailing, and there is no finer area in the world to me. I came up with many ideas for how I could make this dream of mine reality, the majority of which involved running restaurants in ludicrously unviable locations (I'm not sure what it is about me that wants to run a catering business where there are no people). In comparison to some of my early ideas, a restaurant on Canna – still probably one of the hardest places to stock and staff in the UK – seemed like quite a sensible, solid one.

The ferry stops over for a few hours on a Sunday, and that was all the time it took to make the decision and commit. Next thing you know, you're fresh-faced off the ferry and taking in what you've just taken on. There was a community meeting the day I got here. Held in the shearing shed, it was the first time I'd sat down with the whole island (any whole island, for that matter). These were the people I was about to start a new life with, and I've never looked back. I absolutely love it.

We're a close community and when it comes to your plate of food, just like our parties or the maintenance of the island, almost everybody is involved. You'll see the pots in the bay, just outside our door, from which Peter and Craig haul the seafood. The meat comes from the cows and sheep grazing the fields around us, raised by Murdo, Gerry, Cazbo and Isebail. From the hills above, the rabbit man gets (yup . . . you guessed it). Over the wall Indi keeps the polytunnel producing, and the vegetable patch and orchard are tended to by Liz and Pete – who also plays the tunes of an evening. Even the look of the place, from the octopus that surrounds you in the toilet to the design of our beer label, comes from our resident artist, arm-wrestling champion 2022 and fancy dress party insister, Anna.

In times of need many residents have worked in the restaurant, sometimes turning up for a nice drink and being plucked unawares

into the kitchen. We're all in it together, and collectively we each play our part in ensuring the bar stock revolves regularly.

In the following chapters we'll take you through our favourite ingredients, and how to collect, prepare and enjoy them just like we do on a daily basis. When we began our foraging journey, the gap between the available literature on identification, collection and preparation – and a finished dish – was enormous. Many of these ingredients, common and easily collectable, as they can be, are sometimes unfamiliar. We're going to try to make each one feel approachable, with easy-to-follow guides to collection and preparation, and some tried-and-tested recipes to show you how to get stunning meals from simple, highly available produce.

Our recipes come from the Café Canna kitchen, inspired by what is outside our door – those that are in this book are some of our (and our customers') absolute favourites. We really hope you enjoy them, too!

Peter and Craig, the fishermen

Cazbo, Murdo and Gerry, the farmers

Pete playing the tunes

Indi and Liz in the vegetable plot

HOUSEKEEPING

Oven temperatures

Oven temperatures given are for non-fan-assisted ovens. Reduce by 20°C for fan-assisted ovens.

Servings

I always find serving numbers to be on the stingy side in recipes. Perhaps I'm just greedy. Mine are often given as a range – from what I would want, to a 'standard' serving, so you can take your pick.

Foraging

I mention this later in the book, but it's probably worth saying more than once, and quite plainly: I don't necessarily know what I'm talking about. Being self-taught and with many a tale of almost catastrophe to dine out on, please take my advice but also apply your own caution. Always bear in mind that the sea, the shore and foraging in general are not without their own risks. Make sure you know for certain that anything you eat is what you think it is and is safe to consume. Seaweed must always be fresh and attached (see relevant section). Eating raw seafood and seaweed can be very dangerous, depending on the water quality, season and all sorts of other things. Correctly identifying land plants and fungi is essential in avoiding anything from an upset stomach to a bit of death. Ooft, bit of a downer, but it needs to be stressed! Also remember that researching and familiarising yourself with the ingredients within this book is as interesting as it is healthy and fulfilling – with some caution, you can enjoy these gorgeous ingredients that can improve and lengthen your life, too!

Suppliers

If you don't happen to live on a remote Hebridean island, don't worry – there are many local producers who can supply the wonderful ingredients I've mentioned in the book, so you can use them wherever you are.

Food from the Shore, the Sea and the Land

Every dish at Café Canna is made from scratch from produce gathered on the island. But before I get too far it is probably worth stressing that you need not worry – unless you really want to, there is no requirement for you to gather these ingredients like we do. Please don't swan dive into Leith harbour, knife in mouth, in search of kelp – or pounce on a rabbit in the local playpark to skin it with your bare hands. We're very lucky on the island – I can stand at the door and point at what goes into our dishes. Quite likely within arm's length of the bar you can have a chat with the person who collected it, too. However, everything (I think) in this book can be sourced from alternative suppliers. Some of the wonderful ingredients in the recipes – seaweed particularly, gorse and wild garlic – are also very abundant, so if you do find yourself in the vicinity of them at source, you'll soon be able to spot and collect them.

Throughout the book I explain a bit about the ingredients used in the recipes, focusing on the ones you may not have dealt with before. When I arrived on Canna, I didn't know the island, or how to run a professional kitchen, or, in fact, a catering business very well (at all, really). But when I got off the ferry and looked over the bay with a wide-eyed stare at what I'd just committed to (and immediately after that 'I'm-the-only-one-not-wearing-wellies' feeling), the next thought was: what can I eat?

It took a while to get used to some of the produce. I took the ingredients one at a time, learning about each of them – the prep involved and how to find them at their best. I studied how to get the most out of a crab, then what to do with its shell, and what sea lettuce is – and where, when and how to find a crop worth getting soaked for. On this journey, some simple advice really helped, and other things I had to find out for myself. Nobody tells you, for instance, that it's best not to listen to music whilst picking crab, or that dulse exists in quantity at the exact same depth as the height of your wellies, or how to harvest gorse without shredding your hands. Or to never ever joint rabbits with a hangover. But they should!

So I encourage you to get out and try it. There's a stunning larder

Our famous platter and seaweed salad

out there, and it's all free (I'm Aberdonian, so very happy days indeed). Just don't muck it up for anyone else – that's the only rule (well, and don't poison yourself – more on that later). Buying, catching and foraging have responsibilities attached to them that are increasingly important to observe, so please, please do.

One final word of warning before we get started. I'm not what you might call an obsessive when it comes to Latin names or botanical groupings; being self-taught, and with a blinkered emphasis on food, my focus has always been on finding ingredients, less so performing an in-depth biological study. I don't want to be flippant, it's just that I'm going to describe things in a way that is hopefully the most straightforward, if sometimes a little bit technically incorrect. Seaweeds are algae, but I might call them plants, for instance – or they have fronds, but descriptively it might make sense to say 'leaves'. Hope it's useful to you, too.

THE SHORE

Seaweed and Forageable Seafood

Foraging is a real pleasure. Of all the areas to enjoy it, the shore is my firm favourite. I'll go into the specifics of collecting each of our most used and loved seaweeds in a bit, but first a word about foraging in general.

As abundant as it can seem, it is vital to only take what you need and only then what will be sure to regrow. Don't be greedy, now. It's difficult to imagine the world running out of kelp – it is abundant and one of the most sustainable substances on earth – but dulse, pepper dulse and sea lettuce in particular tend to grow in limited areas. Don't take more than a third of it, and most important of all take scissors with you and snip off the fronds. Never pull the whole plant away. This way you can be sure it will regrow and keep producing year after year.

Also, be careful. The shore is an amazing – and amazingly slippy – place. I've fallen into the sea countless times, stabbed myself with scissors through the back pocket more regularly than it would seem normal not to have learned from yet and, maybe most serious, got a lot colder than I realised at the time. Dip in and out is my advice, and have somebody with you: you get somebody to carry the bags and they get a good laugh. It's a fair swap.

All of the seaweeds that I've used – and many more – can be purchased fresh, dried or processed and delivered to your door, depending on the season. Seaweed rehydrates fantastically well and so dehydrated is a great way to buy it. The exception is pepper duse, where the dried version is quite different from the fresh product.

The Hebridean Seaweed Company supplies fresh and dried seaweeds, harvested from our very waters. Mara Seaweed also sells dried seaweed from Scottish and Irish waters. There are many other online retailers – try searching for a local supplier.

Seaweed

'Wow, it's actually delicious!'

More often than not, there will be a plate of seaweed in front of the person making the exclamation. Right they are, too – it *is* delicious! I love it when an underdog ingredient surprises.

I mean, a stunning, fresh, big, fat lobster is truly incredible – no surprises there. But seaweed . . . Previous impressions tend to be that it's slimy, brown, smelly and, for many of our guests, was last seen clogging up their anchor. So not immediately appetising and understandably missing from most people's dream menu. But it's been on ours since 2018. Back then we couldn't guess how it would go down. But we needn't have worried – that same starter is still our most popular five years later.

WHY DO WE LOVE SEAWEED SO MUCH?

Well, it's good for you. I have to admit, being extremely tasty and not bad for you is about where my interest ends, but it would be well worth looking into the antioxidant, cholesterol-lowering, vitamin-boosting, blood-sugar-balancing, thyroid-fixing, fat-reducing properties of the stuff, if you're interested.

It's versatile, too. Seaweed can be used just like any other vegetable – to stuff, to garnish, to eat as a main, salad or side. It comes in a variety of interesting shapes and sizes, and is a vegan-friendly way to create an exceptional depth of flavour. Add it to soups and broths and you won't look back. It is highly umami, as they say.

Unlike other vegetables, being easy to store is one of seaweed's finest properties. Easily dried, on rehydration it will return almost completely to form. Dehydrated, you can keep it for a year, no bother. It will keep in the fridge for many days without loss of quality, but many can also be frozen. It's a wonder to behold – you can make a salad with, say, kelp, with a dressing, and freeze it, and it will be back to its original glory once thawed.

It's a divisive ingredient, and, let's face it, that might be a good thing. Carrots are wonderful – they truly are – but are they inherently interesting without doing something to them? Possibly . . . But seaweed definitely is. If you're having a dinner party, it's a really easy, cheap, quick way of adding some 'Oh hey, what's that?' into what could be a standard side dish.

Another reason to love it is, of course, its shear tastiness. To be unapologetically simple, and extremely tasty in all sorts of ways, is a major plus point.

HOW TO FORAGE FOR SEAWEED AND WHAT TO DO WITH IT

Almost all seaweeds, unless you want to dive, require a low tide. This forced timing gets you out in all kinds of conditions. The thought of dipping into a freezing sea on a miserable day is hardly ever appealing from the sofa, but it always ends up being a treat.

Whilst we're at it, do not ever take seaweed that is not still attached and so still alive and growing. Washed up, you have no idea what has happened to it or for how long it has been decomposing.

Once you've collected it, either use it or store it. Many recipes out there (perhaps most of them) use seaweed in flaked or powdered form, which is fair enough – it's a very valuable addition to the larder and one that some of the recipes in this book make use of. We like seaweed to be a respected member of the plate – the star, even. Once you know how to prep it, consider using it in quantity, not just hidden away in a mere sprinkling.

TIDES

When collecting any shore-based food there's no getting away from the tide. There aren't many varieties of seaweed or seafood that you can forage at all tides. It's easy to underestimate by just how much height the sea varies. A couple of metres is a lot of shore, and we see around four metres of variance at times.

You always want a low tide to forage – the lower, the better. That is when the greatest part of the shore is exposed; different species are uncovered at lower and lower points in the tide, so you get more and more choice the further the tide is out.

Tide varies according to the lunar and solar cycle (and many other things), and the bigger the tide, the bigger the variance, so the higher the high tide and the lower the low tide. Spring tides occur every fortnight – these have the lowest low and the highest high. A week after each spring tide is the neap tide, with a less low low and less high high! In practice, this means that around every two weeks, at the dip of a spring tide, is the best time for foraging. The rise and fall is a

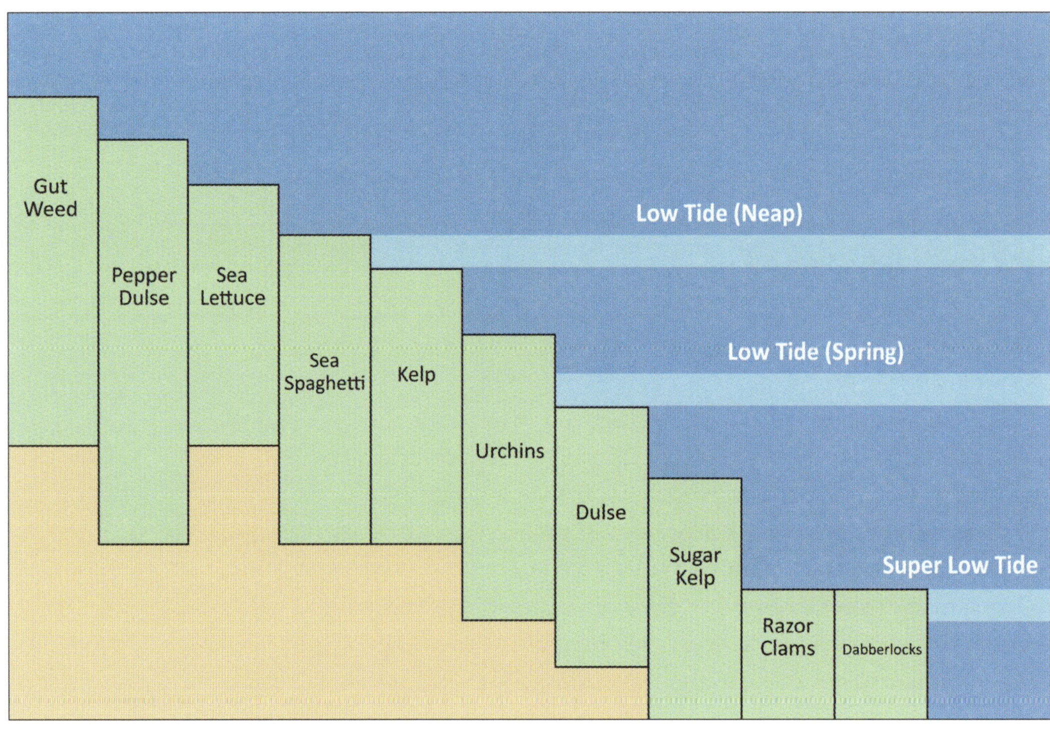

curve, though, so a day or two either side is normally very good too.

This tide talk is all very well for some questionable party chat, but what does it mean in practice? Well, different species become collectable according to this cycle. So even at not particularly low (neap) tides, seaweeds such as gutweed, sea spaghetti, pepper dulse and sea lettuce are within reach without diving. As the lows start becoming more extreme, more and more is uncovered. Kelp and urchins first, then towards the lowest lows dulse, dabberlocks and sugar kelp. Only at the very lowest spring tide (which happens near the equinox), do we normally find razor clams – at least here on Canna.

An app or website is the best way to check and plan for tides. There are many around. I quite like www.tide-forecast.com or the app Tides Charts Near Me (this gives a really handy long-term view). They all work in a similar way, but using Tide Forecast as an example, choose the closest location to you and select 'tide times (30 days)'. The graph will show what I've just described, with the largest variances in the week being spring tide, dropping to the smaller variances at the neap.

So, armed with this information – and noting that unless the app allows you to select your exact location, the tide at your particular spot will be slightly different – you can time your foraging to be at the lowest tides of the month.

HOW TO STORE SEAWEED

We like to use seaweed fresh where possible – not necessarily because it's better but because it saves hassle. We just rinse it and store it in airtight containers in the fridge for two to three days.

For longer periods (up to a year), or if you'd like to use it powdered or flaked, drying it is a good option. You can dehydrate seaweed in a normal oven, but much better is a dedicated food dehydrator (a basic one will set you back £50 to £100). I prefer the versions that have stacking trays to the ones you slide in and out, as they are much easier to load and clean. If you're using the oven, it's the same instructions, just keep the temperature at the lowest setting – you want to dry, not cook, the seaweed.

Drying seaweed

1. Rinse the seaweed in cold water, checking carefully for grit or little crustaceans and molluscs. I find running it through my fingers is the best way to check. Only the fronds (leaves) should be used – any stem should be discarded (ideally only the frond should have been snipped when harvesting). Dulse occasionally has a whitish textured patch on it. This can be easily removed by scraping with the back of a knife (or just cut it out). I don't think it does any harm if you can't be bothered but it can be unpleasant if there's lots of it.
2. Lay a single but tight layer out on each tray. The fronds will shrink a lot during the process, so you want them really snug. Set the oven/dehydrator to 70°C for three hours to start with. You'll need to reverse the order of the trays halfway through that time, as the top one takes longest.
3. Check the seaweed and repeat the process until it is completely crisp to the touch, without any hint of dampness. Be sure – one damp bit can ruin a batch.
4. When done, if you wish to store the fronds whole, place them in an airtight container or freezer bag, date them and store them in a cool, dark cupboard. Another convenient way to store them is as flakes. It's a great way to get the flavour into dishes quickly and easily.

    Make sure the seaweed is bone dry (see step 3), then either in a food processor or, better, I think, a coffee bean grinder, whizz it briefly in small batches. You can store it in a clean jar in a dark place for up to six months. Some of the recipes, such as the smoked dulse butter (pp. 30–31) or the pasta ai funghi e seaweed (p. 61), require it to be flaked first.

Freezing seaweed

Some seaweeds freeze surprisingly well. Kelp, cooked or uncooked, will freeze perfectly. Dulse and sea spaghetti, too. The more delicate varieties – sea lettuce, for instance, or pepper dulse – less so (see the dedicated sections that follow).

THE SEAWEEDS

Canna, and the rest of the UK, boast numerous seaweed varieties. None of them are poisonous, so they are all fair game to the forager and chef. We have used all of them in our kitchen and they each have their strong points. In this section, I'm going to talk you through the favourites – the ones we return to most often – the most versatile, available and, above all as usual, delicious.

Dulse

Dulse, also known as dilisk, lives at the exact point of the tidal zone that is just beyond welly height. There is always a very tempting clump just a little further out than would guarantee dry feet. It is very much worth it, though, and once you find a good spot it is relatively easy to collect large quantities.

Dulse can be found in clumps, clinging to rocks, and – much more prolific, in my experience – growing from the stems of kelp at a greater depth (exposed at around a 1-metre tide on Canna). Once you identify dulse, you'll start seeing it a lot more. It's so easy to collect that I don't tend to bother with the small and delicate stuff growing from the rocks. Go big and find the kelp-attached variety, if you can. You need to scan exposed kelp at low tide to identify it. If you're lucky, it will look like a mophead of red flopping down the top of the stem, beneath the greeny/brown kelp frond. Holding the thick ribbons up to the light is a good way to confirm the colour. The fronds themselves are hardy – almost plasticky. They remind me a bit of the red half of the old cinema 3D glasses – texturally and in colour/transparency.

Dulse can be found throughout the year – but it varies according to season. From spring new growth, which is lighter and more delicate, is more evident. By winter the sea-ravaged fronds have toughened and lost a bit of shine – best for crisps at this point.

Like all seaweed collection, it is bad form to tug the whole plant from its holding – none will grow from that spot again. Instead, take scissors with you, and like a big red mullet give it a haircut that doesn't go to the base. Only remove around a third of it, so that there is sufficient strength left to grow again.

Dulse needs a good check over for beasties.

Smoked dulse butter

We serve this with chunky slices of home-made bread in the restaurant. Smoking the dulse increases its bacon-like savoury appeal and, combined with sea salt and rich, lovely butter, it's a joy to spread thickly and munch.

We package servings in a little parcel. It's a really nice way to store the butter and – we're told – a fun little surprise when opening at the table. To do so yourself, just make the butter as below and wrap in brown parchment like a gift, then tie with twine.

20g dehydrated dulse, finely chopped or ground in a coffee grinder (this would be about 80g fresh)

2 tsp sea salt

50g good quality unsalted butter

First combine the dulse flakes and salt in a large bowl. Cut the butter into two or three chunks then, one at a time, roll in the dulse mixture until thoroughly coated all over.

Kelp

Kelp, before sheep, used to be the big industry on Scotland's west coast and islands. Certainly, the harvesting of it took place on Canna. In those days, it was exported in large quantities for fertiliser and as an ingredient in all sorts of things from soap to glass. These days we are also starting to understand the role kelp plays in protecting our climate and marine ecology, and it is used widely in swathes of supermarket products. Here of course, though, we're interested in it for its qualities as an ingredient.

Finding kelp

Kelp is not hard to find – it is almost everywhere. It's the only seaweed that we don't have specific spots from which to collect it. You can pretty much just go to the nearest bit of sea, at any reasonably low tide, and it'd be surprising if you don't come home with some. You'll see it bobbing around on the surface quite easily. A favourite area for me is a large white sandy area where the islands of Canna and Sanday almost join. It's shallow and wide, and because of the clarity of the water and the colour of the sand you often see other creatures (lobsters, crabs, etc.) scamper by as you tend to the kelp.

Identification and collection

There are lots of varieties of kelp (also called kombu) in the UK. The first and by far the most abundant (and most accessible, as far as Canna is concerned) is oarweed. It has a single frond/leaf that then splits into multiple thinner sections – it's a bit like the sea has ravaged it (which it has). Further out you'll find dabberlocks, with a single long slender frond/leaf and a single spine, and sugar kelp. This is a fantastic ingredient – with a slightly sweet taste, and a pretty and uniquely patterned frond. It looks a little like an escalator at the centre, with ostrich skin-style dimples surrounding that. Many of the west coast gins incorporate sugar kelp into their botanicals – and you can use it much the same as any other variety. On Canna, there is an odd patch of it growing at a very accessible depth, just below the bridge. It's amazing – normally it is out of reach on all but the very lowest tides –

but here you can easily see it sway in the tide.

For cooking, any kelp will do just fine and I'd use them fairly interchangeably. Just don't take the whole plant – cut sections of leaf. Whilst you're still welly deep, run your fingers over the leaf to remove any little beasties – they'd rather stay where they are than take a trip to your kitchen. Then roll it up and stick it in your bag.

Storage

Because of the ease of collection, we rarely find a need to store kelp. It dries very well in the dehydrator but does take a bit of time – three to four hours at least at 70°C. In a sealed container it stays fresh in the fridge for days. Once cooked, it freezes very well for a 'vegetable'.

Wrapping in fresh kelp is an excellent way to retain moisture, and it adds a very difficult to describe umami taste to almost any fish or meat – mackerel wrapped in kelp and roasted is really popular on our menu (p. 74). This is also a great trick for the BBQ or beach fire, where it will keep meat or vegetables moist and seasoned whilst also protecting them from the flames.

The kelps: oarweed, sugar kelp and dabberlocks

Kelp collection at one of my favourite spots

Pepper dulse

When I take people foraging for seaweed for the first time, they often find it hard to see how this greeny-brown slimy stuff we are collecting from the shore can become something of interest in the kitchen. Pepper dulse is a welcome exception to this rule. It already looks kind of pretty, but when sampled in situ – straight off the rocks – it tends to be accompanied by an impressed and enthusiastic 'Mmm!' It's delicious right from the off. There is no mistaking the deep aroma and taste of garlic, with a hint of truffle and sea. It is blatantly food; anyone can see that. With a smidgen of the grandiose, they call it the 'truffle of the sea', which is fair enough. I think it deserves that. Either way, being rich in savoury, salty, garlicy goodness, it is hard to imagine a better accompaniment for seafood.

Finding pepper dulse

Pepper dulse is seasonal. You'll get it over winter, with early spring being the best time to look. By late April it will start to look like a flabby, dry version of itself and in summer may only be found in small, shaded crevices. When you find it, it is one of the easiest seaweeds to collect. If you're lucky – and we are on Canna – it grows like rugs on the sides of large rocks, accessible at almost any low tide.

Identification and collection

To collect pepper dulse, you basically just need to give the rock a haircut. Observe the foragers' code – do not pull, snip. Don't take too much from one area. Don't let the images misguide you – it's a tiny plant. Each frond looks like a spindly red micro Christmas tree. You'll be lucky if it grows an inch or two long. However, as it grows in dense patches, it should be fairly easy to spot. The taste and smell make identification easy. Just watch what else you're snipping along with it – as there are often other species growing amongst it. Most likely is carrageenan – at first glance this will look like a particularly bountiful sprout of growth amongst the patch, but is much more wiry and doesn't have the same flavour.

Storage

I'm afraid the bad news is that what makes pepper dulse special is easy to lose during storage. It's still great either frozen or dried, but it doesn't have nearly the same pungency. The only decent way to capture the goodness is to use it (or eat it) straightaway – combine it with cheese, say (p. 53), so that the flavour is absorbed around it.

It's still a very worthwhile addition to the larder, regardless – it will add a savoury depth to any dish.

To dry it, rinse it in a colander, then spread it evenly on trays in the dehydrator or in the oven. Two hours at 70°C should do it. You'll find that by the end a lot of the fronds have dried up and are so small they've fallen through the tray holes – this is fine, you can scoop them out of the bottom (but check for little creatures). Once completely dry to the touch, seal in freezer bags and label with the date. It lasts for yonks, perhaps a year.

For reasons I'm not sure I understand, pepper dulse tends to get less press in the recipe books than other seaweeds. It is a fantastic accompaniment to any fish or seafood.

Sea spaghetti

It's from the sea and looks like spaghetti – sea spaghetti! This variety is a great gateway to seaweed – it's up there with the easiest to forage and probably the most akin to land vegetables of them all.

Finding sea spaghetti

Up to many metres long, and found in giant manes, it's a very easy one to either spot floating on the surface, or flopped along the seashore when the tide is right out. Sea spaghetti anchors itself to a rock – you often find huge plants that, when traced back to their roots, are attached to nothing but a small pebble. Its long, stringy fronds can be found at quite high ranges of the tide.

Sea spaghetti – on Canna, at least – is available all year round. However, it varies considerably across the seasons. Around March you'll see the new growth – thin, fresh, very green and properly spaghetti-like in size. A quick blanche (literally a second or two) and it's a great noodle replacer or addition to any salad. By April, the fronds will be a lot longer and thicker. More like sea tagliatelle in width now, the vegetable will have real crunch and substance. This is the best time to harvest and use it. It can be boiled quickly to replace pasta and will be robust enough to hold sauce. For the rest of the year the fronds will become progressively wider, growing ever thicker and longer. It's all good and just requires a little more cooking the thicker it is. By the time next March comes along, some of the old growth will still be around, but will by then have become a bit less pleasing to the eye – all withered and hairy (who are we to judge).

Storage

Sea spaghetti will sit sealed in the fridge quite happily for three days. To keep it for longer (and as above, it's well worth storing samples from across the year), dry it. We rinse ours, then coil a strand or two into a circle – a bit like a flat nest – to dry it in the dehydrator. This makes storage a lot more convenient.

Forageable Seafood

RAZOR CLAMS

Called spoots, or spooties around here, there is probably no funnier thing to forage than these. We often take people to look for them, if the timing is right, and it's always a winner of a day. Widely available from coastal beaches, they are absolutely gorgeous to eat.

If you notice broken razor clam shells on the beach, there's a chance that spoots are about. Take note and return at the lowest point of a big spring tide (p. 24). You only get about half an hour, so arrive early, armed with a cup full of salt.

Finding razor clams

You'll only find spooties at the very lowest of low tides. Standing at the waterline, look along the beach. If they're there, and you're lucky, you'll see a thin spurt of water emerge from the sand, about half a foot high. This means you're in business. Go to the hole that the spurt came out of and quietly, crouching down, pour some salt into it – and be ready! The clam should push itself out an inch or so. Grab it! But do not pull it – just hold it there. You'll feel it pull back; just resist that until it tires a bit, then pull it out another few inches and hold once more. Repeat until it fully emerges. It will be dangling a length of weird white willy-ish (it's not a willy) flesh out of the bottom of the shell – this is normal, and it will retract. That's what you'll be eating. Don't lay them directly on the sand or they'll try and burrow away again.

Be responsible – it's easy to wipe out a patch and, once done, they may not return, so only take a few.

My favourite way to eat them is simply steamed in wine (p. 54). However you cook them, though, clean them in plenty of water and treat them like a mussel – they must be alive when cooked. Only use those that are still closed (if not, give them a bang to see if they close up). They can survive for up to a day wrapped in a damp tea cloth in the fridge.

The spoot of the spootie!

URCHINS

Urchins are possibly up there with the most challenging eats. It is possible you may be put off (or are already), so keep this in mind as you read – urchins, in my humble opinion, are probably the finest tasting thing that comes out of the sea. They are properly delicious. Like a creamy, massive, luxurious oyster perhaps. I can't get enough of them.

Urchins are prevalent on our shores – bright white spiky balls from orange to grapefruit size. Getting in amongst rocks that have been uncovered by a low tide is how you find these, usually nestled at the bottom of a rocky little valley.

Eating urchins

I'll tell you how to deal with them before we discuss what to eat and how. It's pretty simple. Using a tea towel to hold the spiky beast upside down, and over a sink, as it will emit water, use scissors or a small sharp knife to carefully cut round its bum-like mouth to create a large hole. Discard the bum/mouth and pour away the contents. Peering inside, you'll now see heaped teaspoon-sized orangy mounds arranged round the centre of the shell. These are its gonads, and that's what you eat . . .

It gets better. To enjoy, scoop out the flesh. This can be cooked and used in recipes, such as our urchin béchamel (p. 50), but the best way (in my opinion, at least) to eat an urchin is raw, no condiments, just like an oyster. Like I say, it can look a bit spongy and unappetising, but it really is very good indeed. (Note: I should probably warn you against eating raw seafood, but it's up to you.)

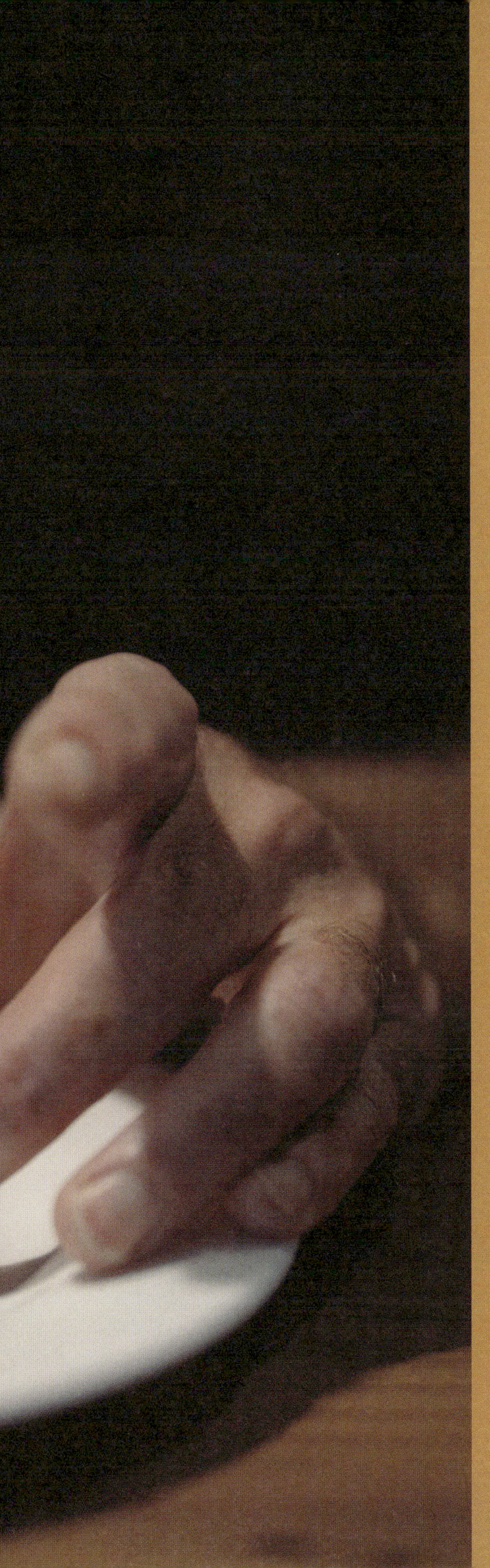

RECIPES FROM
THE SHORE

Kelp salad with toasted sesame oil and rice wine vinegar dressing, and dulse crisps

Sea spaghetti and dulse fritters

Dulse croquettes

Sea urchin béchamel

Pepper dulse and (home-made) crowdie

Spooties

Kelp dashi miso ramen

Pasta ai funghi e seaweed

Moules marinière with wild garlic oil

Laksa with sea spaghetti, mackerel and octopus

Dulse and potato soup

Crispy dulse and egg mayonnaise sandwich

Foraged dulse caviar tartlet, with crab and celeriac remoulade on a pepper dulse shell

Kelp-wrapped whole roast mackerel

Kelp salad with toasted sesame oil and rice wine vinegar dressing, and dulse crisps

Inspired by the ubiquitous seaweed salad found in many Japanese restaurants, this is our most popular starter by some distance. In place of the traditional wakame (also known as Japanese kelp) we use native kelp. For texture and an additional savoury note, top it all with dulse crisps and plenty of sesame and pumpkin seeds.

Once prepared, the kelp in this dish can be used in many alternative ways. Try swapping out the dressing for a simple vinaigrette, use in place of pasta, or stir fry with some other vegetables as an interesting side dish.

One of the beauties of this dish is it can be made in advance (and is better for it). It will store in the fridge with the dressing for up to three days.

———

To prepare the kelp, rinse it under cold water and then, working in sections, roll it up into a fat cigar, then slice it into thin ringlets – about the width of a pound coin. Place all of this into a pan of water and simmer, covered, for about 1–1½ hours (the cooking time is only a guide: the older or thicker the kelp is, the longer the cooking time). Test every so often and extend, if necessary. It should be really tender and easy to bite through. Note: it will get slightly harder when cooled. Drain and let it cool. Whisk the rest of the ingredients well to make the dressing, then combine with the kelp thoroughly.

To prepare the dulse crisps, there are two options. If using dehydrated seaweed, you can deep fry it for just a few seconds, or heat some oil in a pan and fry until crisped up. If you are using hydrated or fresh dulse, then first of all do not deep fry it! It will splatter dangerously. Instead, rub oil into the seaweed and place it on a rack in the oven at 160°C for 3–4 minutes until crisp. Set aside at room temperature. The crisps will go soft after a day.

Plate up the kelp salad, sprinkle with your seeds of choice, if using, and then lay the crispy dulse on top.

Serves 2

For the salad

200g (approx.) kelp, fresh or rehydrated (that's about 30g dehydrated)

2 tbsp rice wine vinegar

2 heaped tsp sugar (soft brown ideally) or honey

2 tsp ginger, grated

¼ tsp cayenne pepper

2 tsp soy sauce

1 tbsp toasted sesame oil

¼ tsp salt

For the dulse crisps

a few lengths of dulse (at least finger length, but the longer the better), fresh or dehydrated

sunflower oil

To garnish (optional)

2 tbsp pumpkin seeds

2 tbsp sesame seeds

(feel free to swap in seeds of your choice)

Sea spaghetti and dulse fritters

Serves 4, as a generous starter

150g self-raising flour

2 tsp chilli flakes

1 tbsp white wine vinegar

150ml ale (any ale or lager)

salt and freshly ground black pepper

100g fresh or rehydrated sea spaghetti, chopped into 2-inch lengths (approx. 40g dehydrated)

70g fresh or rehydrated dulse, roughly chopped (approx. 20g dehydrated)

½ red onion, finely sliced

1 tsp ginger, grated

sunflower oil, for frying

These make a fantastic 'beer snack', or a nice textural addition to Asian brothy soups – like our ramen dish (p. 57).

Sea spaghetti is a really easy seaweed to find and prep – see the dedicated section on it. Here, it is woven with other vegetables and fried to create a satisfying crunch. We like to serve it with a simple soy or chilli sauce.

————————

Combine the flour, chilli flakes, white wine vinegar and ale, with a good seasoning of salt and pepper, to form a batter.

Mix in the sea spaghetti, dulse, red onion and ginger.

Heat oil in a deep pan – ensure it's deep enough to submerge large dollops of the mixture. It's hot enough when a drop of batter sizzles in it.

Scoop up a large spoonful of the mixture and use another spoon to push it into the oil – repeat until you have filled the pan, leaving plenty of space around each.

When golden (about 5 minutes), remove and let them drain on kitchen roll.

Serve straight away with a sauce of your choice – soy or sriracha is delicious.

Dulse croquettes

There is no finer way to burn the top of your mouth than with a good croquette. Ideal with a drink or as a starter, they are crunchy, oozy and flavoursome. In the restaurant we serve them as a trio to represent the land, sea and shore of Canna. Each one represents what is seasonal and good at the time – smoked mackerel, local beef brisket and dulse, say.

Along with the dulse variety, I've included the smoked mackerel too. The dulse ones are often the favourite of the three – a really meaty-seeming vegetarian option and a great way to get the best out of the flavour of this fine sea vegetable.

Whilst a little involved to make, we often prepare croquettes as a team. We form a conveyor belt and have a little laugh and a gossip as we go. Make the béchamel and then add either the dulse or mackerel to the mixture.

Consider making this dish over two days if convenient – leaving the filling in the fridge overnight ensures it is nice and chilled before assembling the croquettes (which makes it a lot easier). They store very well, so it's a good idea to make a decent batch.

To make the béchamel filling, fry the onion in the butter for 10 minutes until soft and slightly brown but not burned. Add the garlic and cook for a further minute. Add the white wine and reduce the mixture down to an emulsion – it'll take 20–30 minutes. Add the flour and cook gently for around 40 seconds.

Start adding the milk, bit by bit, stirring vigorously all the time until the milk is used up. Simmer for 5–10 minutes or so, letting it thicken. Mix in the mustard, nutmeg and salt, then let it cool.

If making the dulse croquettes, add in the chopped seaweed to the béchamel filling and refrigerate for at least an hour or overnight.

Makes 10–12 croquettes (around 3 per person is about right for a starter)

For the béchamel filling

1 small onion, finely chopped

35g butter

1 clove garlic, finely chopped

100ml white wine

25g plain flour

200ml milk

1 tsp Dijon mustard

a pinch of nutmeg

1 tsp salt

250g dulse (fresh or rehydrated), roughly chopped, or 200g smoked mackerel (1–2 fillets)

To assemble the croquettes

100–200g breadcrumbs – dry some white bread in the oven, then whizz to a crumb in a food processor. If you are buying breadcrumbs, try and get panko.

50g plain flour

3 eggs, beaten

If making the smoked mackerel croquettes, once the béchamel is cooled you will add the fish. Remove the skin from the mackerel and flake it, being careful to remove any bones, then combine.

You are now ready to assemble the croquettes. Lined up together on your work surface, you want (in this order): the bowl of mixture, a plate or tray with flour in it, a wide bowl with the eggs that have been beaten with a fork, a plate or tray with breadcrumbs, and an empty tray or board for the finished croquettes. It's best to work in batches – spoon out 4 or 5 dollops of the mixture into the flour, ensuring they do not touch. Then roll them around until semi-coated. At this point pick each up and form into a tighter ball.

Using a fork, and one at a time, place into the egg and move around until fully coated, then plonk into the breadcrumbs. Use the fork to move the croquette around before finishing by moulding it into a cylinder shape in your hands and giving it a final roll. Ensure the ends are covered too. Place in a single layer on the final board. When all are done, cover and place in the fridge (or freezer – they cook from frozen fine).

These are cooked half in the frying pan and half in the oven, so first warm your oven to 200°C, then heat a few inches of sunflower oil in a pan (if you are using a deep-fat fryer, heat the oil to 160°C). Carefully place 3 or 4 into the pan and fry until golden (about 4–5 minutes), then remove from the fryer and place in the oven for a further 6 minutes. Serve immediately with aioli.

Sea urchin béchamel

Serves 4

4 sea urchins

100g unsalted butter

1 small onion

50ml white wine

2 tbsp plain flour

250ml whole milk

4 tbsp breadcrumbs
(optional)

The urchins that dot our lower shore are stunners – big, fat, spiky jewels of the sea. At the right tide, they are very easy to collect as well. They are much more widely available in fishmongers now too, so one way or another they should be within reach of the keen seafood fan.

I cannot recommend urchins enough; they are beyond gorgeous. Eating them raw (the preference for me) can be a challenge for some. This simple recipe is a good compromise – quick and easy, yet bursting with the distinctive oyster-like creaminess of urchin.

Half the urchins. Use a tea towel to protect your hands from the spikes, and as carefully and as neatly as possible cut cleanly around the circumference of the shell (sharp scissors tend to work best). Once you have an opening, pour the liquid that is inside into a bowl (we'll use it later). See page 39 for instructions on how to extract the gonads – the spongy blobs that line the inside of the shell. Wash the side of the shell that doesn't have the mouth (if serving in the shell).

Melt the butter and gently fry the onion (do not let it colour). Once soft, add the wine and let it reduce for 5 minutes. Add the flour and stir for 2–3 minutes. Add small amounts of milk at a time, stirring as you go to create a thick, creamy sauce.

Add the chopped gonads to the sauce and add a little of the retained liquid – enough so that it just coats the back of a wooden spoon.

Pour the sauce into the four cleaned shells, sprinkle the breadcrumbs on top (if using), and bake at 200°C in the oven for 5–10 minutes, until piping hot and lightly browned on top.

Pepper dulse and (home-made) crowdie

One of the great travesties of pepper dulse is that its immense flavour is easily lost when it's heated or stored, so this really simple recipe makes the very best of it.

Crowdie is a traditional fresh Scottish soft cheese. It's delicious and extremely easy to make – it requires a few hours of non-attendance and about 5 minutes of actual work. It's a great little recipe to have up your sleeve. It can be used in place of many soft cheeses – soft goat's cheese, brie or even cream cheese. Any of which you can also switch in here.

Freshly made crowdie keeps well for a few days at least.

Quantities aren't too important once you've made the crowdie.

Serves 2–3

1 litre milk

juice of 1 lemon (3 tbsp)

salt and freshly ground black pepper, to season

2–3 tbsp double cream

a handful or two of pepper dulse

Combine the milk and lemon juice in a pan and warm it so it's almost simmering. It should reach 80°C, but not much more – do not let it boil. The milk will start to separate into curds and whey (clumps start to form). Once the process has started, let this carry on for around 5 minutes, then remove from the heat and let it cool until it's just warm.

You want to strain out the curds (the whey is useful too, but we're going to discard it for this recipe). To do this, line a colander or large sieve with a clean muslin or, failing that, a tea towel, and suspend that over a bowl. Pour the contents of the pan into the strainer you just created and let it drain like this for at least 2–3 hours. Remove the cheese from the cloth, season with salt and pepper, and mix in the cream until you're happy with the consistency.

Rinse the pepper dulse and pick through it to ensure there is no sand or debris remaining. Keep a couple of nice pepper dulse pieces for garnish and chop the rest roughly. Mix the chopped pepper dulse through the crowdie (or alternative cheese, depending on what you are using).

Serve with toast or oatcakes – perhaps even a little chutney!

Spooties

Serves 2

a good glug of olive oil

1 shallot, finely sliced

1 clove garlic, finely chopped

a good glug of white wine

4 razor clams, thoroughly
cleaned in fresh water

1 tbsp parsley, finely chopped

Spooties (or razor clams) are an absolute crowd pleaser when you go to forage for them. Happily, they are also one of the more gorgeous items to put on a plate. Meaty and rich, their flesh is not dissimilar to scallops in texture – if cooked well. Like mussels and many other seafoods, they are best cooked lightly, with the difference between amazing and tough as boots being all too close.

———————

Heat the oil in a frying pan (ideally, with a lid, or else use tin foil).

Add the shallot and garlic, and sweat them on a medium heat, stirring constantly.

Add the wine and turn up the heat, then add the clams and cover.

Leave for a minute or two, then check. As soon as the shell opens up, they are ready.

Remove from the pan and separate the meat from the shell. Cut away the dark intestinal sack about halfway up and place back in the shell.

Pour over the remaining liquid and garnish with parsley.

Kelp dashi miso ramen

Our ramen is served in big bowls, heaped with noodles bathed in a densely flavourful, creamy miso broth. The toppings vary, but often include teriyaki sweet potato, crispy dulse, a pickle of seasonal veg or seaweed, a sea spaghetti fritter and an egg (from our nice new chickens). It is vegan friendly (if you omit the egg and use non-traditional but great rice noodles).

The dashi – in this case, made from kelp and dried mushrooms – is an incredible stock that comes in numerous variations, but, as a family, form the foundations of many Japanese dishes. You may not taste it in the finished dish, but the intense depth it provides will be missed if it is omitted.

There are plenty of substitutions that are possible here, but the miso and the dashi are deal breakers – I don't think there is an alternative for them. The bean paste is not often stocked in supermarkets but can be easily ordered online – or substitute black bean paste at a push. The toppings can (and should) change with what is available. When there is purple sprouting broccoli in the plot, for example, we fry that with the teriyaki sauce in place of the sweet potato. The fritter is entirely optional. It works equally well with oat milk instead of soy milk.

However you decide to make yours, you'll enjoy a hearty, healthy, slurpy experience – one that is surprisingly quick and easy to put together time after time.

———————

Start with the kelp dashi, as this should infuse for as long as possible. Place the dried kelp, mushrooms and cold water into a pot and leave (off the heat) for at least 30 minutes to let the flavours develop, ideally overnight in the fridge.

Meanwhile, get some (or all) of the toppings ready – the crispy dulse and hard boiled eggs should be cooked, and (if using) the seaweed fritters prepped (see overleaf).

Serves 2

For the kelp dashi

3–5g dried kelp (approx. 5 x 10cm)

6g dried mushrooms

360ml water

For the broth

3 tbsp toasted sesame oil

4 garlic cloves, finely chopped

14g (approx. 2.6cm) ginger, grated

2 spring onions, the white part chopped, or ¼ white onion, finely chopped (save the green part of the spring onion to garnish the dish)

2 level tsp broad bean paste, or doubanjiang (or 2 tbsp black bean sauce)

4 tsp (approx. 60g) white miso

2 tbsp vermouth (or sake)

4 tsp soy sauce

1 tbsp tahini

500ml unsweetened soy milk (or oat milk)

240ml kelp dashi (see above)

½ tsp salt

150g ramen (for vegan, use rice noodles)

chopped parsley, to garnish, if using a white onion above

Toppings

2 hard boiled eggs
(unless vegan)

1 handful crispy dulse
(see p. 141)

2 sea spaghetti and dulse fritters
(see p. 44)

**For the pickled kelp
(or other veg)**

2 tbsp rice wine vinegar

a squeeze of honey or maple
syrup

2 handfuls of tenderised kelp,
cut into strips (see p. 74) – or, for
example, carrot or courgette
shavings (use a peeler), or sea
spaghetti

**For the teriyaki sweet potato
topping**

½ sweet potato, sliced
(approx. 1cm thick)

3 tbsp teriyaki sauce (this is
surprisingly easy to make but
obviously you can buy it too)

For the pickled kelp (or other veg), place the ingredients in a bowl
with a pinch of salt and combine, then leave to marinade.

For the teriyaki sweet potato topping, combine the ingredients in an
oven dish and roast at 200°C for 40 minutes, or until soft but
retaining shape/structure.

Once the dashi has had time to infuse, heat it to almost (but not quite)
a simmer. At this point – and this is important, or it will go slimy –
remove the kelp and mushroom, then take it off the heat. You can
slice the kelp/mushroom and add it to the final dish (I usually add the
kelp to the pickle).

Next, make a start on the broth. In a pot, on a medium heat, add the
sesame oil, garlic, ginger and onion and fry, stirring constantly to
ensure the garlic doesn't burn, until aromatic. Add the bean paste and
miso – keep stirring or it will burn.

Add the vermouth and use to deglaze the pan – use a wooden spatula
to scrape anything stuck to the bottom or sides back into the paste.

Add the soy sauce and tahini and combine. At this point, if you are not
using it immediately, you can remove the pan from the heat, cool and
refridgerate.

With the pan on a medium heat, start adding the milk, like you would
stock into a risotto: add a little, combine, then add a little more until all
of it is in.

Add the dashi (note: you should end up with slightly more dashi than
you need – add only the quantity in the broth ingredients) and salt.
Heat through and it is ready to serve.

Finishing the dish

Cook the noodles, either as per instructions or, if preferred, add the dried noodles straight to the broth. This will cause it to thicken slightly (which some people love), but you can use the spare dashi to loosen it up again.

Add the noodles to each bowl, then pour on the broth. Arrange the toppings, trying to keep the dulse crisps on top, and garnish with the green tops of the spring onions or parsley.

Pasta ai funghi e seaweed

Our version of the classic Italian 'mushroom pasta' – with an additional umami hit from seaweed and a hint of miso.

When available, we do this with wild fresh (and dried) field mushrooms in place of chestnut, as we get these on Canna. We've also tried this dish with oyster, porcini and a few others, all with success.

The seaweed too is highly interchangeable – the recipe includes dulse flakes, but it's great to include some that's fresh or rehydrated too, for some vegetation on the plate. Ribbons of cooked kelp work well, as does sea spaghetti and dulse – add any (or all) of these to the pasta in the final minutes.

Personally I like really thick pasta for this – pappardelle ideally, but it's fantastic with linguine too.

———————

Grind the dried mushrooms into a powder (we use a coffee grinder, but a pestle and mortar or blender would also do) and place in a bowl with the dulse flakes and hot water. Mix well.

Cook the pasta in salted water.

Meanwhile, in a large frying pan (eventually everything will end up in here), fry the onion and carrots in olive oil until the onion is nice and soft. Add the garlic and fry for another minute, stirring often. Add the mushrooms and fry until almost cooked through, then add the wine and increase the heat.

Once the wine has reduced to almost nothing, add the miso paste, dried mushroom/dulse liquid, and the thyme, and combine. Add the tomatoes and cook for 10–15 minutes.

Season well and, using tongs, move the pasta into the frying pan with the heat on low. Combine well and, if necessary, add some of the pasta water to loosen it a bit.

Serve with shaved parmesan and lots of black pepper.

Serves 4

40g dried mushrooms

1 tsp dulse flakes (optional)

300ml boiling water

400g linguine or pappardelle pasta

4 tbsp olive oil

1 onion, peeled and finely diced

1–2 carrots, diced

4 garlic cloves, very finely chopped

400g chestnut mushrooms, cut into 1cm slices

50ml white wine

1 tsp miso paste (red ideally, but white is good too)

1 tbsp dried thyme

400g tin chopped tomatoes

shaved/grated parmesan, to serve

freshly ground black pepper

Moules marinière with wild garlic oil

Serves 4 – for a main course,
double the quantities

1kg mussels

25g butter

1 large / 2 small shallots, finely
chopped

1 garlic clove, finely chopped

3 sprigs fresh or wild thyme,
or a tbsp dried

150ml white wine

50ml double cream

4 tbsp parsley, finely chopped

12 tbsp (3 tbsp per dish) wild
garlic oil

Mussels are plentiful on the island and are relatively easy to collect –
you'll find them on rocky outcrops just below the tideline. If foraging,
be sure to collect those that are still covered in water, and it would be
wise to purge them in some clean salt water for a few hours too.
Farmed mussels are (to me) a rare exception, in that they can be
superior to those in the wild. Less gritty, and strictly controlled for
cleanliness, they are a very cheap, nutritious and delicious option for
the home cook.

In the restaurant we often have this recipe on at the beginning of
the season, to be replaced with mackerel when it starts to appear. The
wild garlic oil adds an extra dimension and a fantastically vivid green
to the dish. Serve with some home-made bread to mop up the
goodness.

Start by making the wild garlic oil (see p. 161, for the recipe).

Pour the mussels into a clean, empty sink, along with an empty
colander. One by one, check each mussel is closed; if it isn't, tap it
against the side. It may close then, but if it doesn't, discard it. Pull out
the 'beard' – the tassly bit – then place it in the colander. Once they
are all in there, run the colander under water to clean the mussels.

You can store the cleaned mussels for up to a day in the fridge, with a
damp tea towel covering them (do not seal with a lid).

Place the butter into a pan large enough to hold twice the volume of
the mussels and on a medium heat fry the shallots for a minute. Add
the garlic and fry for another minute, then add the thyme and wine
and continue cooking for 5 minutes.

Turn the heat up to high and add the mussels. Place the lid on top and, holding the lid down with a tea towel, give the pan a vigorous jiggle every minute or so. After around 5 minutes, have a peek. If the mussels have opened, add the cream, replace the lid and it give another jiggle. Immediately plate up into bowls, then sprinkle with the parsley.

Dot each bowl with around 3 tablespoons (or more, to taste) of wild garlic oil and serve with home-made bread.

Laksa with sea spaghetti, mackerel and octopus

Our take on the slurpy, spicy, sour, richly fragrant Malaysian classic, served with toppings sourced from around us. Definitely some ingredients that are not exactly native to the island, but lemongrass, for instance, stores extremely well in the freezer, as does shrimp paste, so it's kind of 'Canna meets the mainland'.

———————

Create the paste by placing all the ingredients, plus a few tablespoons of water, in a food processor or blender and whizz until smooth.

Add a few tablespoons of sunflower or other neutral oil to a pan and, when hot, add the paste. Fry, stirring all the time, until aromatic, then add the broth ingredients and simmer for 10 minutes.

Prep the additions. Place the noodles in a bowl and cover in boiling water. Place the mackerel and octopus on a tray and roast for 10 minutes. Use a potato peeler to make strips of courgette or cabbage. Blanche the sea spaghetti in boiling water for 2 minutes.

After 5 minutes, add the noodles to the broth and, when soft, plate into bowls, using tongs to place the noodles, then pouring the broth over them. Arrange the mackerel, octopus, courgette or cabbage strips, lime halves, sea spaghetti and egg around the bowl. Garnish generously with fresh mint.

And slurp!

Serves 4

For the paste

2 garlic cloves, coarsely chopped

2 red chillies, deseeded and coarsely chopped

5cm fresh ginger, peeled and finely grated (or more, if you prefer)

1 small onion

¼ tsp ground turmeric

2 stalks lemongrass, sliced

2 tsp shrimp paste

4 kaffir lime leaves, chopped

For the broth

600ml coconut milk

6 tbsp soy sauce

4 tsp sugar

600ml veg stock

Additions – use some, all or experiment with your own

250g rice vermicelli noodles

4 mackerel fillets (see p. 83)

4 octopus portions (a tentacle or two per bowl – see p. 97)

½ courgette, diagonally sliced, or a handful of shredded red cabbage

2 limes, halved

4 handfuls of fresh or rehydrated sea spaghetti

2 boiled eggs, halved

a handful of fresh mint, chopped

Dulse and potato soup

Serves 4

100g fresh or rehydrated dulse (about 30g dried), roughly chopped

2 potatoes, peeled and cubed

a good glug olive oil

1 tsp lemon juice

1 litre whole milk (or oat milk, if vegan)

salt and freshly ground black pepper

This hearty broth showcases a traditional Hebridean use of dulse – an ingredient that was much more commonly used in the past, particularly around the Small Isles.

Most of the soups we do are vegan – in this recipe, you can substitute milk for oat milk, no problem. It sounds terribly on-trend to do so, but oat milk is a great alternative and can be easily made at home. It is basically just whizzed up porridge, so who knows – maybe they made this soup back in the day, too.

Place the dulse and potato into water and bring to the boil. Simmer until the potatoes are just cooked, then drain in a colander.

Place the empty pan back on the heat and add the olive oil, potatoes, dulse and lemon juice.

Add the milk and bring to a gentle simmer. Once heated, you can blend it for a smooth soup, but I prefer it chunky and rustic so leave it as is.

Season and serve with good bread (p. 213).

Crispy dulse and egg mayonnaise sandwich

Dulse – when crisped up – is salty, savoury and bacon-like. It is fantastic in all sorts of dishes. We have included it in several other recipes in this book – we use it a lot.

In an egg sandwich, the added meaty smokiness, plus the addition of a textural crunch, brings a huge amount of extra deliciousness.

We're lucky enough to have our own hens, but, if that's a push for you, obviously the more organic and free-range the eggs, the better.

———————

First, boil the eggs for 8 minutes. When cool enough to handle, peel the eggs and mash with the mayo, mustard and chives.

To make the crispy dulse, rub the dried seaweed strips with oil and a small amount of salt, then fry until crisp in a hot frying pan.

Place the egg mayonnaise and the crispy dulse between the slices of bread and enjoy!

Makes 2 fat sandwiches

4 eggs

3 tbsp mayonnaise

1 tsp Dijon mustard

1 tbsp chopped chives (optional)

1 handful of dried dulse strips

a glug of olive oil

4 slices of soft white bread (for our bread recipe, see p. 213)

salt, for seasoning

Foraged dulse caviar tartlet, with crab and celeriac remoulade on a pepper dulse shell

Serves 6

3 heaped tsp white crab meat per tartlet

2 heaped tsp brown crab meat per tartlet

For the pepper dulse shell

50g plain flour

3g sugar

1g salt

10g egg yolk

5g dried pepper dulse (or other seaweed), crushed or roughly ground

8g olive oil

20ml warm water

1 egg yolk, for glazing

For the celeriac remoulade

200g (about ¼) celeriac, grated

180g mayonnaise

4 tbsp lemon zest (about 1 lemon's worth)

4 tbsp lemon juice (about 1 lemon's worth)

2 cloves garlic, crushed

salt and freshly ground black pepper

This is a light, flavour-packed expression of the best of our (or, I would say, *any*) island ingredients. The delicate seaweed shell and juicy dulse caviar topping represent the shore; celeriac represents the land; and, of course, crab is the sparkling sea's contribution. It's one of my favourite dishes and a proud thing to be able to put together from a wild larder.

There are a few components here, and there's no getting around it: together they make it time-consuming to prepare. The (vegan) dulse caviar, is optional, but is a very fun thing to make – you will be mesmerised as the droplets form – so it's worth giving it a bash for that alone. You'll need a squeezy bottle with a thin nozzle, suitable for dripping liquid through, or a pipette or syringe without a needle.

You can mix and match most of this, though, removing elements to make it ever more simple (even just shop-bought tartlet casings and no dulse caviar), yet still delicious, or you can go the whole hog and go for the full recipe, as served in the restaurant.

Other seaweeds make interesting options to replace pepper dulse – anything flaked, basically. These shells, stored in an airtight container, will last a week, but they also freeze very well.

First, make the tartlet shells. We use 4-inch mini tart tins, with a loose bottom. Mix everything, except the egg yolk for glazing, and knead to a smooth dough. Wrap in cling film and refrigerate for at least 30 minutes.

Roll out thinly on a floured surface, then cut out a circle a few centimetres larger than the tins.

To avoid having a tin bottom stuck in the base of the shell, sandwich a tin bottom between two tops. Place the rolled-out dough on top, then add another tin bottom and top over the dough and push down to sandwich it. Trim excess dough. (See photos 1 and 2 on p. 72.)

Weigh down the middle before baking (we use ramekins or espresso mugs – see photo 3). Place all of the tins, with their weights, on a baking tray and bake at 150°C for 50 minutes.

Remove from their casings. If still slightly damp, bake for another 10 minutes without the tin. (See photo 4.)

Glaze by brushing with the egg yolk. Place upside down back in the oven for 5–10 minutes.

Next, make the celeriac remoulade. This is easy! Combine all of the ingredients, season and set aside. You can refrigerate this mixture for up to 4 days.

Finally, the dulse caviar. Place your vessel of oil in the freezer. You'll be dropping liquid into this later, so the container needs to have a wide top. Leave for about an hour – it should become thick and gloopy but not freeze completely. Keep an eye on it. If it does freeze, it'll defrost in the time it takes to do the next step.

For the dulse caviar

1 litre sunflower oil in a large, sealable jar or vessel (the oil can be reused once you've finished)

20g ginger, roughly sliced

30g dulse (pepper dulse is amazing for this, too), ground into flakes

2 tsp soy sauce

20–30g beetroot, roughly chopped

3g agar-agar powder

Add 450ml water to a small pan, along with the ginger, dulse, soy sauce and beetroot, then bring to a simmer. Turn off and steep for 30 minutes.

Usually, I take a loose approach to measurements, but this part requires precision – a lack of accuracy from this point is the difference between juicy, shiny caviar and rock-hard ball-bearings (or slush).

Place a sieve over a measuring jug and pour exactly 400ml through it into the jug. Empty and rinse the pan, and put the reserved 400ml back in.

Whisk in 3g of agar-agar and bring to the boil, whisking often. Boil for 2 minutes, then decant into the bottle with the nozzle. Leave to cool for 5 minutes.

Remove the oil from the freezer and ensure it is gloopy but not frozen. Very slowly, pour/drip from the bottle into the container, moving around the surface as you go. If things are going to plan, caviar droplets will form and gently fall and gather at the bottom of the oil. Once your oil container is about a quarter to a third full of 'caviar', stop.

Pour the caviar into a sieve, capturing the oil for re-use. Leave to drain freely for a good few hours. Place the caviar in a jar and refrigerate for up to a week.

To construct the tartlets, start by filling the shell with the celeriac remoulade – to very nearly the top of the side. Put a good teaspoon of brown crab meat in the middle, then cover and surround that with white crab meat, creating a hillock of crab.

If adding caviar, create a slightly flat area on the peak and very carefully spoon a little on, ensuring that it sits up on top – it's easier to take time to do this in a oner than spend time picking out caviar from the crab.

Serve immediately (the casing will soften after a few hours).

Kelp-wrapped whole roast mackerel

Each mackerel serves 1

1 mackerel, cleaned and gutted

1 fresh or rehydrated sheet of kelp, about the size of a standard envelope – enough to wrap around the main body of the fish, with its head and tail sticking out. If you only have smaller strips, just use a few and overlap them.

Wrapping any fish or vegetable in kelp is a fantastic way to protect it from heat, keep in the moisture and infuse the dish with a subtle savoury, sea-like kelpy note. We often use this technique for cooking on beach fires or barbecues. It also works really well for roasting in the oven.

There are two options regarding the kelp. You can use it in its raw, hydrated state, which will give a stronger taste. It's the way to go if you are going to barbecue the mackerel. The other option is to tenderise the kelp before wrapping the fish in it – this gives a lighter taste, but has the advantage that the kelp is edible and a bit crispy after cooking (this is how we do it in the restaurant).

If you've bought or caught the mackerel whole, then you can follow our filleting steps on p. 83.

————————

If you need to tenderise the kelp, simmer it for approximately 1 hour until very soft, then stop the cooking by cooling in water. You can store it for up to 2 days.

Preheat the oven to 210°C. Place a sheet of greaseproof paper on a baking tray. Roll the kelp around the body of the mackerel, then place it on the tray with the overlap facing down.

Roast for 15 minutes (small fish), or 20 minutes (big fish).

To serve, use tongs to carefully lift up the fish parcel and plate it up. We serve this with a rhubarb, cannellini bean and potato bake (p. 219) and a side of veg (p. 223).

THE SEA
OB 147

Fish and Seafood

Craig landing today's catch

We have a long-serving fisherman who has been known since anybody can remember as 'the red man' (he has a red boat). He's also called Peter. We communicate daily with him, as we also do with incoming yachts, via VHF. The red man is an accomplished and opinionated cook, and so our long 'over' interspersed conversations are often about food. He's helped us out in all sorts of ways over the years and is as passionate as we are about the produce – he is as important to our operation as anything else. Frustratingly, sometimes, he won't sell a fish unless it's still physically flapping at our door – that's his level of commitment to freshness. He'll often turn up at the kitchen, usually at the frantic peak of service, proudly offering a culinary challenge from the depths.

Happily (for us and the bunnies) our local (and now former) rabbit man Craig is fishing our waters, too. Trained by the red man, it's an amazing thing to have islanders working the seas that surround Canna and the restaurant. We all love and respect what comes out of the sea and know how lucky we are to be dealing with it – so everything Peter and Craig get is line-caught or creel-caught, and so completely sustainable.

Mackerel

Even I can catch a mackerel, such is the prevalence of them in our seas. Healthy, delicious and versatile, I wouldn't swap them for any other fish. Pop the line down, pull it up, ten mackerel! Spend an hour and a half untangling the line, then repeat. Another ten mackerel! It's a great way to spend the day.

If you don't have the red man or Craig on the other end of a VHF, or don't have access to a spot where you can fish them yourself, you can buy them really fresh from most fishmongers for most of the year, as the season will move across the UK. If you hold a fresh mackerel by one end, it should remain horizontal, and have clear eyes, firm flesh and a shiny exterior. It's not the best to buy or keep frozen, that's all – it's absolutely fine, but you will lose a touch of the magic.

The season has varied dramatically over the last few years, but they're normally around for most of the summer season here. They're great for just about anything: roasting, pan-frying, barbecue, paté or, our little ritual with the first one of the season, sashimi.

We often combine mackerel with seaweed (see kelp wrapped, p. 74, and stuffed parcels, p. 122), a satisfying sea-and-shore collaboration, and a brilliant one for a beach BBQ. It makes a wonderful taco, too (p. 107). A firm favourite.

We have a friendly seal in the bay that is more than partial. If you're on a boat and have caught a few, give him a treat, eh? He will love you for it.

Eating mackerel

Mackerel has a bad, boney reputation for being tricky to fillet, and maybe that's fair enough, but with simple techniques they are quick and simple to prepare.

An obvious option is to cook it whole. I think it's just such a treat to devour a fish in its entirety. Where possible, I'd go this route.

If eating whole, the only step (and your fishmonger may well have done this) is to gut it (if you're storing freshly caught fish, make sure you do this before it goes in the fridge). Turn the fish over and cut

When Jane the carer came
mackerel fishing . . .

through the skin (about 1cm) in one long straight line from its bum to
just before its head. Pull out all the gunk from this cavity and discard
(although you can fry up the roe if there is any – it's delicious), then
rinse out. Job done.

However, sometimes you want a filleted fish and that's not so hard
to do either (see overleaf).

Storage

Whether freezing or refrigerating, ensure that the whole fish has been
gutted first.

You can store them in the fridge for two to three days. They
should never smell fishy, and it's definitely a fish that the quicker it's
eaten the better.

Mackerel don't freeze amazingly well – one of their only
weaknesses. If you need to, it's not a disaster – however, one method
to try is freezing them in water, creating blocks of mackerel.

Step-by-step guide to filleting a mackerel

1. **Start with the head.** Create an incision down the sides and across the top, just behind the head. Start on one side and cut down from the top to the bottom immediately in front of the pectoral fins. Repeat on the other side, then cut across the top to join the two cuts.

2. **Removing the head and guts.** At this point you should be able to grab the head and pull it down and away from the body, so that the top comes away first, and if done in one motion much of the guts should be pulled out along with the head. Bin all of that.

3. **Removing the fillets.** A flexible fish or paring knife will make the next bit much easier, but you can get away with a nice sharp kitchen knife. With the fish on its side, and the head end facing you, hold the body down with a flat palm. Work the knife from front to back, scraping along the top of the back bone as you go, until the top fillet is removed. Turn it over and repeat for the second fillet.

4. **De-boning the fillets.** Once you have your two separate fillets, we now need to pin bone them. Tweezering mackerel bones is a mug's game – more often than not you'll tear the flesh into an ugly mess. I'd recommend the following approach – it's so much easier and produces a much neater fillet.

   To remove the central line of bones, have the fillet 'head' towards you. Run the point of the knife along one side of the central line of bones towards you – from almost the tail right off the edge of the head end. The knife point should almost but not quite go through the skin. Repeat on the other side of the central line of bones. You should now be able to grab the central strip of bones at the far end (easiest done with boning tweezers) and pull it towards you. Done correctly, the strip of bones remains intact, coming away to leave a clean channel behind.

   Finally, there may be some stragglers, particularly around the 'head' of the fillet. Either tweezer these out, or again probably easier is to use the knife – in this case, just run it horizontally below the bones to slice them away from the fillet. As a final check, run a finger in both directions along the fillet. You can feel for bones much more easily than looking for them.

Crab

Around here, crabs come in a few flavours.

Velvets – the ones you may have netted off a pier as a kid – make an excellent stock or bisque. They're also a fun snack, simply boiled and picked. I truly wish to find another use for them, but so far have not.

Brown crab, however, is another story. For me, a simple whole brown crab with a mixing bowl-sized portion of aioli is the ultimate meal. Seriously flavourful, rich and delicious – and possibly a little easier to deal with than you might think. They are tremendously valuable creatures (but surprisingly cheap to buy).

Whole, uncooked crabs should be used when alive – store them covered with a damp tea towel in the fridge, or in seawater if that's an option. Once cooked, they will keep for two to three days in the fridge. The meat freezes reasonably well – for three months.

Not all crab dishes require them to be picked – Singapore chilli crab (p. 104) is an amazing dinner party dish to dig in and share with friends; a proper food experience. It's so messy it needs to come with a warning, a stack of napkins and unlimited finger bowl refills.

Picking the meat out of crab is not difficult or challenging – it's the kind of simple activity that creates a pleasant form of thoughtlessness, even. I've detailed the steps, but when planning to do this, remember to use the shells as well. It would be criminal not to.

Crab bisque (p. 150) is a stunning dish that almost comes for free. Make the stock at the very least, so as not to be wasteful – it freezes well.

Crab meat, once retrieved, has vast uses. We've taken some of the dishes from our menu into this book – there is the crab tartlet (p. 70), crab linguine (p. 126) and ravioli (p. 101). Not in the book but well worth mentioning, a sandwich to be savoured: add a touch of mayo, lemon, a pinch of cayenne and some crab meat to sliced, home-made white bread.

Buying crab whole can be considerably more cost effective than buying pre-picked meat. The processing involved in commercial crab meat renders it less flavourful, too. Purchase them alive and make sure the claws are banded or disabled before continuing. On the islands we

all know somebody with a crustacean war wound! A good crab feels surprisingly heavy for its size – indicating plenty of meat inside.

Male (cock) crabs are identifiable by a smaller flap underneath. They have larger legs and claws, and so more white meat. Female (hen) crabs have less white meat, but larger bodies, so more brown meat. The process for preparing them both is exactly the same.

Eating crab

Cooking requires consideration. They're fine, fascinating creatures – so it seems fair to go about things in a way that doesn't risk excessive harm. We encourage everybody to try and be as familiar as possible with how food arrives on a plate – and starting from alive is an important step. Advice differs, so to some extent, just like lobsters, you need to decide for yourself.

Many chefs will tell you that putting a live crab into boiling water will kill it faster and with less fuss than trying to dispatch it first. Common advice now is to subdue it first by cooling – in the freezer, for example – down to 2°C to 3°C, rendering it in a semi-subconscious state. To be really sure, with the crab upside-down place a sharp knife through the nervous system by lifting the flap at the back and slicing through there, then doing the same from the cavity at the very front, just behind the mouth. Unpleasant for sure, but if you're still hungry, let's continue!

Crab can be cooked in many ways – they are great on the BBQ or roasted, for instance, but all of the recipes in this book go with boiling. You need a pan with about twice the height of the crab of water on a vigorous, rolling boil. The water should be well salted – to something akin to seawater (in fact, seawater is great for this, if you're happy with where it came from). Out on the boat we always use that. Place the crabs in, lid on, and leave for 15 minutes if small, and more like 20 if very large. Some recipes recommend you leave the crab on the boil until it's floating, but I don't think that is particularly true, especially if there's more than one in the pot.

Just before the time is up, prepare a vat – a pot, or sink perhaps – of cold water which you'll plunge the crab into when done. If you're picking the meat, it's best to get the body really cold. If you're going to either serve it whole (see p. 121) or continue with a recipe, you just need to get it cool enough to handle. Then it's time to get the stock on, if you're doing that (see crab bisque, p. 150), and clean up.

Step-by-step guide to prepping a crab

1. **Preparation.** Like many things, there are two levels to crab-picking – normal
    and obsessive. There is an exponential difference in time between a 90 per
    cent and a 100 per cent yield. When it comes to the labyrinth of tiny
    intricate tunnels of flesh in the body or the smaller segments of leg, the
    compromise is that if left behind this flavourful meat will contribute to your
    stock or bisque instead. You'll need a teaspoon, a hammer (ideally a kitchen
    one, but I guess anything will do) or the back of a large knife, a chopping
    board, a seafood pick or other long pokey thing (a chopstick or cocktail
    stick, say), a tea towel, a knife you don't care about much and a metal
    receptacle each for the white and brown meat. Metal is the best for this
    task. I also keep close by a large pan for the shells, ready for making the
    stock. The most important thing: be absolutely sure no tiny bits of shell end
    up in the meat. This is why the receptacles should ideally be metal – each
    piece that you add should be thrown in and if you hear a 'ting!' you know
    that a piece of shell has got in. Unfortunately this makes a quiet, music-free
    and podcast-free environment the best.

2. **Start with the legs.** Twist off at the base. It may bring some of the socket
    with it (a good but not vital thing). Unless particularly large, I usually only
    bother with the first section (the 'thigh', if you will). Holding that thigh
    section 'knee' down, tap the middle of it with the hammer. There's a knack
    to this: you're aiming to create a split down the length of the section, not
    obliterate it. Twist that section off at the joint and you should be able to
    prise it open to pull or poke out one piece of meat the length of it. You can
    do the same with the other smaller sections of leg if you have the time and
    inclination.

3. **Next, the claws.** Start furthest from the pincers and, section by section,
    bash to expose the meat. Try and remove it whole. Lay a folded tea towel
    on your board and, holding the claw, with the section furthest from it flat
    on the tea towel, fold the towel over and tap increasingly powerfully until
    the shell cracks. Use the teaspoon and pick to scoop out everything you
    can, keeping the meat in the largest chunks possible. Move on to the next
    section. When you get to the actual claw, lay it down and bash it in the
    middle. The shell should come away relatively easily. Running down the
    middle of the nice big chunk of meat you'll find a strip of hard
    bone/cartilage – just slide the meat off it.

4. **Separate the body from the carapace.** Twist off the flap on the underside (you may need to prise it open with a knife). Remove the carapace (the widest upper shell section of the body). With it on the board, upside down and facing away from you, place your two thumbs on the ridge that's on the lower portion of the body at the back. Hold the carapace lip from behind with your fingertips and lever your thumbs up. The top will come away, exposing the innards.

5. **Remove the dead man's fingers.** These are the four or five squelchy grey finger-shaped gills on each side. They're not poisonous but are foul (I've tried) so get rid of them.

6. **Remove the face.** Taking the top shell, with one last indignity to the crab, push the face in until it comes away inside the shell. Attached to the face there are some hard innards and the dark stomach sac, so get rid of all that. Make sure no dead man's fingers end up in the top portion, otherwise everything – no matter how unappealing it might look right now – should be kept. Set aside.

7. **Scoop and scrape all of the meat from the top lid (carapace).** This is your brown meat. Be sure to dig in under the lip to get everything out.

8. **Remove meat from the leg/claw sockets.** Pick out any white meat reachable from the leg sockets. If there is still a knuckle in there, lever it out to widen the entrance. The claw sockets particularly are well worth a shot.

9. **Finally, the body.** Some of the best, sweetest (and hardest to get at) meat is in the body. On the top, in a sort of wide groove that runs down the middle, there can be a good deal of meat. Scrape it out with a teaspoon, then cut the whole head in half lengthways. Now exposed are some thin channels of meat that can be picked out with varying success (remember you can justify leaving some for the stock). Another option is to take a fork and dig into the newly exposed sides. You can easily push through the channels, and whilst this meat will have too many bits to use, it can – as is – make a very satisfying crunchy/meaty snack for the chef (I'm partial to it).

Lobster

We don't know how lucky we are, living in an environment so rich with these fine beasts. Lobsters are one of the simplest meals to cook, but there are some golden rules.

Freshness is paramount. Make sure it's alive when you get it (and when you go to cook it). Whole, uncooked lobsters can be stored covered with a damp tea towel in the fridge – or in seawater, if that's an option. It'll flap its tail enthusiastically when picked up, if it is alive. In the restaurant we keep the time between sea and plate to just moments. It's why you'll sometimes see a staff member running towards the pier mid-service.

Good ones feel heavy for their size – indicating muscle and meat density.

Cooking time needs to be judged correctly. Cook it quickly and simply – it's one of those ingredients that the less you do to it, the better. Once cooked, store for two to three days in the fridge. The meat freezes reasonably well, for three months, so if you can't use them immediately, cook and freeze them.

And that's about it.

Eating lobster

Cooking a live lobster is not humane and should be avoided. There are two options. One, subdue it by placing it into the freezer for 15 to 20 minutes (make sure you don't freeze it entirely, though). Two, slice through its head to kill it instantly. To do this, take a large, sharp knife and position it, blade facing forward, on the 'X' mark near the middle of the top of its head. In one motion, holding the body firmly with the other hand, plunge it down, through the head, and with the tip still on the board, pivot the knife forward and down to slice through the front of the head. It will wriggle for some time afterwards, but it is dead.

Cooked simply – we often flash-roast ours, a great way to seal in the moisture and flavour, whilst also short on mess and pans – with a side of chips and garlic mayo, it's difficult to beat (see p. 129). Or do something fancier in advance, like our ever-popular tartlet that combines elegance with comfort (p. 111).

Langoustine

Langoustine – or simply prawns, as they're known around here. We sell them by the pint glass during the day and, sitting out on the benches, with the sun bouncing off the water, a glass of chilled Albariño, a nice salad, mayo and some home-made bread, a very pleasant afternoon awaits.

Like lobster, buy them alive. Nice and fresh, they should set off spontaneous mayhem in their container when knocked. Watch their pincers – they nip alright! Either handle them by the tops of their body or by both their arms at once. They can rear up and nip you if you only hold their tail. Or, as the red man mockingly said to me once, why don't you use some tongs? Quite.

Store them alive for less than a day in the same way as lobster – covered with a damp cloth or seaweed, in a cool or refrigerated spot. You really have to use them fresh and alive, but if you really have to store them, they are best frozen (whole or peeled) after cooking.

Langoustine come in three standard-ish sizes – smalls have tails that are kind of pinky-sized; mediums are more like large thumbs; and large can go all the way up to ridiculous. As lang's ma arm, as Robert Burns would say. The bigger they are, the more they cost per kilo.

There isn't really any prep. Use them simply, as per the recipe on page 133, or a big favourite here is the home-made prawn toast (p. 108).

Step-by-step guide to peeling langoustine

Everybody has their way, and most will swear it is the best. A common approach is to squeeze the tail to break it, then peel back the sections to remove. This can be slow, and it can damage the flesh (and splatter juice everywhere). Our preference when working through a bucketload is as follows:

1. Lay the langoustine down flat.

2. At a join slightly forward of the middle of the tail, push the side with your thumbs to break the shell horizontally, then break that same join back on itself to split the shell.

3. Next, pull away the tail end of the shell.

4. Pull the meat out of the other half.

Octopus

It has to be said that fishermen around here don't get on very well
with octopus. They are surprisingly abundant, and renowned catch-
thieves – adept at stealing the creel contents before it can be lifted. It
was with some glee that the red man first appeared at the kitchen
door offering one and has been encouraging their inclusion on the
menu ever since.

Octopus around here are hardy. It takes a lot to tenderise them.
Freezing is actually a good start – not only is it a reasonably humane
way of killing them, but it also helps to break down the tissues. It is
best to defrost octopus in a bowl of cold water.

Prepping an octopus

If it's whole, you'll need to clean the octopus. Start with the head. Grab the body with one hand, and place the fingers of your other hand under the lip at the bottom of the head. Pulling with your fingers, you want to peel the head back until it's inside out and removed from the body completely. Anything that's not the white outer bell-shaped flesh should be discarded. That is unless you want to do something with the ink – which is in obvious dark sacks. Put these aside, if so.

Separate the tentacles by cutting just below the eyes and discard the upper messy bit. The legs should still be attached to one another. Push your thumb through the central hole to remove the hard beak if it's still there.

Put a pan of water onto the heat. Once boiling, add the octopus. The person that taught me this insisted that a cork must also be placed into the pan to ensure tenderness. Science disagrees, I think, but out of respect for tradition I sometimes do it anyway.

Simmer for 45 minutes at least. You know it's done when a knife easily cuts the flesh. Try it on one of the thickest sections of leg. If it doesn't slice easily, continue to simmer until it does.

At this point it should be tender and ready to include in many dishes. You can store octopus in the fridge for two days, the freezer for two months.

Our Octopus salad (see p. 114) is a nice, simple dish to try – and an easy and impressive starter. Or you can fry or grill the tentacles in a slosh of red wine vinegar, which is delicious.

RECIPES FROM THE SEA

Crab and crowdie ravioli with crab bisque

Singapore chilli Canna crab

Mackerel tacos

Langoustine (prawn) toast

Lobster macaroni cheese tartlet

Octopus salad

Crab doughnuts

Octopus ballotine

Whole crab

Stuffed mackerel parcels, with cauliflower puree, sautéed dulse and dulse butter

Crab linguine

Whole lobster

Langoustine – as they are

Langoustine and smoked haddock pie

Spice-roasted whole mackerel

Smoked paprika and garlic mackerel, with crispy dulse

Lobster, crab and langoustine lasagne

Home-smoked mackerel

Pan-fried mackerel sandwich with tartare sauce

Crab bisque

Crab and crowdie ravioli with crab bisque

If you're going to use crab in a dish, you really need to let it shine. This recipe combines two of the very punchiest uses of it: it is a dish that comes from somebody who really loves the stuff. It takes a little bit of time but makes a seriously impressive starter out of relatively small amounts of ingredients.

Making your own pasta isn't just for the show-off cook – the improvement is noticeable (and the process enjoyable, I think). Ravioli creation is also a fun thing to do as a group. You ideally need a pasta machine (and a little practice). We'll go through how to make pasta with minimum faff – and if you don't have the machine in your kit, you can get away with a rolling pin. If you're lacking in time or will, I guess you can get some very nice ravioli in the shops now, so it would still be a great starter paired with the luscious bisque.

Serves 2 (approx. 6 ravioli)

300g 00 flour

3 eggs

100g white crab meat (see p. 87 for picking)

100g brown crab meat (see p. 87 for picking)

200g crowdie (see p. 53), ricotta or mascarpone

500ml crab bisque (see p. 150)

1 spring onion, the green end finely shredded, to garnish

Start with the pasta. Tip the flour out onto a surface in a wide volcano shape. Crack the eggs into the centre and use a fork to whisk until yolk and white are combined.

Using your fingertips, incorporate the flour into the egg, working from the outside and trying to hold off the egg breaking free for as long as possible. Keep at it until a dough has formed.

Knead the dough by stretching it out using a palm, then folding it back in and repeating. It will probably take 10 minutes – it should be smooth once you're done. Refrigerate for 30 minutes.

Next, first prepare the filling. Mix the cheese and crab. It is important that it's not too wet – remove any excess moisture by letting it drain in a sieve.

Clear as large an area as you can and make sure your filling is ready to go. Heavily sprinkle a tray with more flour to hold your finished creations.

If using a machine, feed the dough through on the widest setting, then fold the pasta in half (as in, back on itself) and feed through again. Repeat this four times.

Keeping the work surface and dough lightly floured. Now, without any folding, go to the next notch on the machine and put the dough through, then repeat through all of the settings until probably the thinnest (ours is 0.9mm – it's really thin, you can sort of see through it). Working to whatever length will fit the available space, lay the created sheets out in pairs of equal length.

If you are using a rolling pin, make liberal use of flour and in much smaller sizes – aiming for sheets the length and width of a whisky bottle, say – roll out the dough as thin as possible without it breaking, roughly in pairs of equal length. Don't worry if it's not perfect – it'll still be great, just cook for a bit longer. The important thing is no holes.

With your sheets of pasta prepared, and making sure they are floured underneath (test that they move) add the filling, about half a spoon of brown crab meat and half of white in a line along your prepared sheet, leaving two to three finger widths between each.

Take another sheet (the second of the pair) and drape that loosely over the one with fillings. Create the ravioli by securing the pasta around each filling, sealing the two sheets and pushing the air out as you go. It's best to start at the back and work round either side of the filling before a final shape and air removal at the front.

Leaving a bit of lip (it's good to give a bit of lip), cut the ravioli into squares or circles.

Place in the floured tray and turn after 10 minutes to ensure they dry slightly all over or they will go soggy. They should form a dryish 'skin'. Ravioli freeze very well – if not using within hours, this is your best bet.

To bring it all together, place the bisque in a wide pan with the lid on, on a medium heat, and bring it up to just simmering.

You have two choices with the ravioli. Safe option: Add the ravioli straight into the bisque and cook for 4–5 minutes. If one bursts, rather than being ruined, some bisque will just have seeped into it, which is fine. Standard option: Bring a separate pan of water to the boil and place the ravioli in for 3–5 minutes. In both cases, you can test if the pasta is cooked by notching a tiny bit off the lip.

Carefully remove the ravioli and plate up (ideally in wide, pre-warmed bowls). Pour the bisque around the pasta, sprinkle with shredded spring onion and serve.

Singapore chilli Canna crab

Although I've promoted messy eating elsewhere in this book, this dish here is the top of the game. We literally serve it with a warning – and if you're cooking it for friends or family, you sort of need to know that they enjoy this kind of thing.

The crab is served in its shell, but in small enough pieces to not need tools (much). Covered in a sweet, sticky but fresh and lively chilli sauce, it's a really fun way to eat – and definitely one to share. That way you're all in it together.

This is our version of the classic, but using our native brown crabs. Serve in a big bowl in the middle of the table with some flatbread. It's really easy to prepare and massively enjoyable and fun to eat.

———————

First, prepare the crab. Follow the cooking and prepping instructions on pages 86–89. Use the back of a knife to bash each section of the claw legs. Don't obliterate them: ideally they should be whole but cracked enough to be easily pulled apart by hand. Cut the body, small legs still attached, into four quarters.

Over a medium heat, add a good glug of sunflower oil to a large pan and add the shallots, shrimp paste, garlic, ginger and chilli flakes. Move it around constantly to avoid burning. When aromatic, add 500ml water, the ketchup and the soy sauce, and stir well.

Scrape out the brown crab from the carapace, add that and increase the heat.

Add the crab pieces and fry for 5–10 minutes, ensuring they are thoroughly coated and heated through.

Serve the pan directly to the table for sharing, or decant into a large bowl, garnishing with the spring onion and coriander.

This goes well with flatbreads – and don't forget the napkins!

Mackerel tacos

This is the very first dish that went on our menu at Café Canna. It is
incredibly easy to reproduce at home and actually very healthy. This is
a universally loved way to enjoy a brilliant fish.

If you've bought or caught the mackerel whole, then you can
follow our filleting steps on page 83.

We serve these with spiced sweet potato fries – you can make an
approximation of these at home by roasting wedges and dusting
them lightly with cumin and salt once they've crisped up.

———

First, prepare the toppings. Mix the chipotle paste into the mayo
thoroughly. In a separate bowl with some spare space, toss the
shredded red cabbage with 1 tablespoon of the chopped coriander,
along with a glug of olive oil and the juice of half the lime (divide the
other half into wedges to serve).

Next, make the tacos.

Mix the spices in a bowl to create the rub, then coat the fillets in the
spices. Heat a small amount of sunflower or other neutral oil in a
frying pan and place the fillets skin side down in the hot oil. Let them
crisp up (3–5 minutes), then turn over for a further 30 seconds to a
minute. By that time, they should be cooked. Remove from the heat
and keep them warm in the pan.

Heat the tortillas, either in the microwave or, better, scorch them over
a naked gas ring burner. (Hold them with tongs!)

Pile the red cabbage on to the tortillas, followed by the fish and some
chipotle mayo. Scatter the remaining coriander over the top and serve
with a wedge of lime.

Serves 2

1 tsp chipotle paste

2 tbsp mayonnaise

¼ of a red cabbage, thinly
shredded

2 tbsp coriander, finely
chopped

a few glugs of olive oil

1 lime

1 tsp cumin powder

1 tsp chilli powder

1 tsp garlic powder

4 mackerel fillets

4 mini (approx. 5 inch)
tortillas

Langoustine (prawn) toast

Serves 4, as a starter

200g langoustine meat,
peeled and cleaned
(very roughly 800g whole
langoustine)

1 garlic clove, peeled
(don't bother chopping)

3g ginger, peeled

1 egg white

½ tsp caster sugar

1 tsp soy sauce

2 spring onions, roughly
chopped

4 thick slices white bread,
crusts removed (our white loaf
is really good for this, and it's
a great way to use up slightly
stale bread. See p. 213 for the
recipe)

a few glugs sesame oil, for
brushing

1 egg, lightly beaten with a fork

100g sesame seeds

sunflower oil (or veg oil),
for shallow frying

sweet chilli sauce (optional),
to serve

A big staff favourite, this recipe came from our collective love of talking about food.

During the season – beyond the Small Isles Games, when we travel to neighbouring Eigg, Muck or Rum to compete in inter-island welly throwing, sheep racing, tug-o-war battles and drunken ceilidh dancing – we rarely get the chance to leave the island. Towards the end of these stints, our chat regularly turns to what we're going to eat when we set foot on the mainland. A good (and sometimes bad) Chinese takeaway is always up there. The inspiration for this dish came from such a conversation.

If you can't get fresh langoustine, you can substitute regular prawns.

———————

First, peel and clean the langoustine. See p. 94 for instructions.

Whizz the prawns, garlic, ginger, egg white, sugar, soy sauce and spring onions either in a food processor or in a jar that a hand blender fits into fairly snugly.

Brush one side of each slice of bread with sesame oil, then spread the prawn mixture on top of that. A good thick slathering, all the way to the edges. Brush the top and sides with the beaten egg, then, over a plate, sprinkle liberally with sesame seeds.

Heat the sunflower oil in a frying pan (chuck a sesame seed in to see if it sizzles), place one or two slices in with the prawn side facing up. Leave until slightly browned, then turn over (spatula and tips of fingers work best for me) and cook, prawn side down, for a further 2–3 minutes.

Cut each finished slice in two diagonally and serve with either soy or sweet chilli sauce (my preference).

Lobster macaroni cheese tartlet

My favourite sailing food, without question, is the carbohydrate celebration that is the macaroni pie. Available in all good Scottish bakers (and see p. 205 for our own version), warmed up on a cold active day there is no finer antidote to a chilly breeze.

Here we take that humble thug of a snack and spruce it up for a dinner party. It is important that the lobster is loud and clear in every bite – this recipe shows you how to get the very most out of its flavour.

———

First, make the pastry. There is often a load of faff and fear in shortcrust recipes. This is tried and tested to always work. Make sure the butter isn't rock hard (microwave, if so) – it should be nice and soft. Mix the flour, butter and a few pinches of salt in a mixer, or use your hands – rubbing between finger and thumb – until it looks like chunky breadcrumbs. It doesn't need to be perfect. Lumps are OK.

Pour in half the water and continue to mix (still using the machine, if you were), then add the rest. At this point it should have come together into a robust dough that will hold its shape if cut in half. If too wet, add more flour and mix; if too dry, do the same with water.

Give it a little knead with your hands on a clean surface (you shouldn't need to dust with flour, but do so if it's sticking). After kneading for a minute or so, it should have all come together into a smooth ball. Ideally, place in the fridge for an hour to a day, but we happily use it straight away as well.

When you are ready to make the tartlet filling, start with the lobster. Put on a large pan of heavily salted water and bring it to the boil. Kill the lobster humanely. Boil the lobster whole for around 7 minutes, then remove it and put aside. Keep the water in the pan.

Makes approx. 12 tartlets

We use 4-inch mini tart tins with loose bottoms, but muffin trays could work well too. Or rather than individual portions, you could create a full quiche-sized version and slice later.

For the pastry

450g flour

200g butter (at room temp.)

salt

90ml water

To make the tartlets

1 medium lobster, approx. 800g (ideally alive – see instructions on p. 90 – but you can use a cooked one too)

400g macaroni

2 onions

50g unsalted butter (salted is fine, too, just adjust seasoning)

4 garlic cloves

½ tsp cayenne pepper

200ml white wine

50g plain flour

1.1 litre milk

2 tsp English mustard

310g cheddar, grated (we use Isle of Mull or Kintyre) – save 100g of this for the top.

Cook your pasta in the same water, but for a couple of minutes less than the instructions on the packet. It should have a bit of bite still.

Sweat the finely chopped onions in butter for 5–10 minutes, then add the garlic and cayenne for another 5 minutes or so. The onions should be very soft, but not browned.

Add the wine and increase the heat to boil off nearly all of the liquid. Lower the heat and beat in the flour, followed by the milk and mustard to produce a white sauce. Remove the sauce from the heat and add in the grated cheese.

Remove the meat (and juice) from the lobster. Twist the head off, adding any juices within to the sauce. It might not look delicious, but the stuff in the head is what is going to add most of the lobster flavour, so do not skip.

There is a lot more meat than you think in a lobster. Crack the claws and remove the meat. To get it out of the spindly legs, use a rolling pin to roll and squeeze it out of one end, a bit like getting toothpaste from the tube. From above, cut lengthways down the middle of the body and extract the meat. Discard the dark intestine that runs the length of the body. At the very bottom (surprisingly) you'll find the anus (probably attached to the intestine) – get rid of that too. Everything else is fair game for inclusion. Once you have collected the meat, chop it into thumbnail-sized chunks.

Add the meat and the pasta to the sauce. It might be best to add the pasta a bit at a time – it should be a very saucy mixture, not solid with pasta. Allow to cool, and refrigerate if not using that day.

Remove the pastry from the fridge. If it's too hard to work with you can microwave it for 30 seconds or so. Roll it out quite thinly – about the same thickness as a 50p. Place over and into your buttered tartlet cases – press into the base so that all of the pastry is against the sides. You can then roll the rolling pin over the top to remove excess.

Fill with the sauce, ensuring there is visibly lobster and macaroni in each. Sprinkle with more cheddar.

Cook in the oven for 30 minutes at 180°C.

Let the tartlets cool until you can handle them. Remove from the cases and cool on a rack.

Octopus salad

Serves 3–4

1 octopus, cooked and prepped

1 red onion, finely sliced

a handful of parsley, finely chopped

1 red pepper (or any other colour), thinly sliced

1 garlic clove, very finely chopped (optional)

100ml olive oil

100ml white wine vinegar

salt and freshly ground black pepper

This simple, lovely recipe was taught to me by a Portuguese lady who worked on the island for a summer. It's important to note that our octopus are more difficult to tenderise than their Mediterranean cousins (those with the two lines of tentacles on each leg). Prepared using the method on page 97, this is a guaranteed win.

———————

Combine the finely sliced red onion, parsley, pepper and a little garlic, if you like.

Combine the olive oil and white wine vinegar and season well.

Separate each octopus tentacle with a knife and chop the head into thin slices. Add to the veg and mix in the dressing.

Serve cold, with some bread.

Crab doughnuts

Savoury mini doughnuts, bursting with a zesty crab filling – airy and light, yet also, well . . . doughnuts, so satisfyingly bad as well.

These are best enjoyed immediately after they've cooled; however, you can make the doughnuts ahead of time. They last a day or so in an airtight container.

Melt the butter and let it cool for 5 minutes. Add the butter and all the other doughnut ingredients to a bowl/mixer and combine thoroughly. Let the mixture rise for 2–3 hours.

Roll the dough to approximately 3cm thickness. Cut into circles using, for example, a scone cutter (4–7cm).

Pour enough oil into a pan to reach about three times the height of the dough rounds. Heat to 180°C – hot enough to make a breadcrumb fizzle.

Deep fry a few doughnuts at a time for around 4–5 minutes, or until golden brown, placing them on a paper towel to dry once removed. Test the first one to ensure it has cooked through. This will give you an idea for the rest. Let them cool.

Mix all of the crab-filling ingredients together, then slice the doughnuts almost all of the way through to form a mini-bun and cram as much filling as possible inside.

Makes 20–30 mini doughnuts

For the doughnuts

60g butter

90ml water

150ml double cream

1 egg, beaten

460g plain flour

57g sugar

1 tsp salt

5g instant yeast

sunflower oil, for frying

For the crab filling

200g white crab meat

30g good mayonnaise

a pinch of cayenne pepper

1 lemon, juiced and a few scrapings of zest

Octopus ballotine

Serves 4

3 octopus, prepared and cooked
(see p. 97, for instructions)

a splash of olive oil

a splash of balsamic vinegar

a splash of cider vinegar

2 tbsp parsley, finely chopped

salt

1 tsp red chilli flakes

This is a really beautiful way to serve our fisherman's friend, the octopus. It is a great 'make-ahead' starter for a dinner party. Just be sure you have a sharp knife – it is absolutely key to this dish.

Lay out a double length of cling film, wider than the longest tentacle stretched out. Separate each of the tentacles by cutting between each at the base. Lay them lengthwise, placing some on top of the others, the idea being to form a vague sausage shape. Lift the cling film up and around them, and roll the cling film to create a solid cylinder.

Twist the ends so it looks like a sort of Christmas cracker – keep twisting to tighten it. Pierce the skin a couple of times to let out some juice, then tighten it up again.

Wrap with more cling film and refrigerate overnight.

Just before serving, slice the octopus into thick discs – perhaps three per person – and remove the cling film. Plate it up and drizzle with olive oil, balsamic and cider vinegar, and sprinkle with parsley, salt and chilli flakes.

Whole crab

The best way to eat crab is to treat it as an experience. One that may take hours – it's a long meal spent earning the unbelievably delicious nuggets and enjoying the indulgent rewards of the really chunky bits. It's messy and fun – and with the freshest crab, and the right cooking time, no chef can produce something finer.

We get brown crab around the island of Canna – always good-sized, occasionally colossal. We sell them by the crab rather than the weight, and every so often a customer gets surprised with an absolute whopper. Chance dictates that sometimes this is somebody who has never tried it before. There have been shrieks of terror at the scale of the undertaking. Fear not, though – it is a simple task, one that we have become adept at talking people through over the years.

Sides should be equally simple. Personal preferences abound here, but a surprisingly large amount of aioli or good mayonnaise, some home-made bread (see p. 213, for recipe) and a straightforward salad (see p. 220, for ideas) are the go-to for me.

Prepare the crab, following the cooking and prepping instructions (see pp. 86–89).

To present the crab, we like to plate the two sides of the body first, with the legs facing one another. Place the carapace, turned 90 degrees, over the legs and between the bodies, so that it slots down the middle. Then balance the two claw legs on top, claws wide open and in the air (like they just don't care). It takes a bit of trial and error, but using the inner edges of the carapace and each other, they should stay in place. Always a precarious one to carry across the dining room!

Serve with your choice of sides and some tools – ideally a pick and a cracker. If you don't have these, or alternatives, bashing up the crab more before serving is an option.

Stuffed mackerel parcels, with cauliflower puree, sautéed dulse and dulse butter

For the cauliflower puree

1 large cauliflower

a good glug or two of olive oil

salt

200ml approx. double cream

For the mackerel parcels

2 tbsp capers, chopped

juice of 1 lemon

small bunch leaf parsley, chopped

1 garlic clove, finely chopped

1 tsp Dijon mustard (use less if substituting in other mustards)

8 large mackerel fillets (avoid piddlers – you need a good size to stuff)

4 strands (about 30cm long) sea spaghetti to tie the fish, plus spares (optional)

For the sautéed dulse

200g fresh or rehydrated dulse, roughly chopped

a glug of red wine vinegar

freshly ground black pepper

This is an impressive and hugely flavourful dish – and a good way to refine the look, if your diners might not like a whole fish staring back at them. These mackerel fillets are stuffed with salsa verde, then tied back together with sea spaghetti to form elegantly packed parcels. The herby zing inside complements the oily firmness of the surrounding fish. Cauliflower puree is a smooth, creamy indulgence – amazing with any fish dish – and it's all finished off with a savoury, almost meaty, dulse butter.

You can easily get away without the dulse butter (for recipe, see p. 31) and the sautéed dulse can be swapped for a nice side of veg (for suggestions, see p. 223). The cauliflower puree, dulse butter and mackerel parcels can all be made in advance and kept in the fridge for three days.

First, make the cauliflower puree. Remove the florets and place on a baking tray with a slosh of olive oil. Season with salt liberally – a teaspoon or four – trying to coat much of the florets.

Cover tightly with tin foil, roast at 200°C for 1½ hours – give the tray a vigorous shiggle about (no need to take the tin foil off) at around halfway. If they're not very tender by the end of the cooking time (you should be able to squeeze the floret bases easily), back in the oven they go until they are.

Once ready, place into a food processor. Add a little cream and blitz, adding more and more cream little by little until the consistency is creamy and silky. If it looks like it's starting to turn to liquid, stop. Check the seasoning and put to one side.

Next, create the mackerel parcels. To make the salsa verde filling, mix the capers, lemon juice, parsley, garlic and mustard together to form a rough paste. Slather the paste on one mackerel fillet (on the flesh side), filling the central channel left by the boning. Place the second fillet on top.

Slide a piece of sea spaghetti under the fish from the back and tie on top in a bow. These parcels keep their shape well, so the loop doesn't need to be tight or particularly strong. Do the same at the front, so you have two neat ties, and chop away any excess.

You can either time the cooking of these parcels with the roasting of the cauliflower for the puree, or store in the fridge for now and heat everything when ready. When it's time, place the fish parcels on a small baking tray with the dulse butter spread between them. Roast for 15 minutes at 200°C.

Meanwhile, create the dulse side – heat some olive oil in a frying pan,
then add the dulse. Move it around regularly and, once almost cooked
– about 5 minutes – toss in the red wine vinegar and some pepper.

Plate up a mackerel parcel with some cauliflower puree and the
sautéed dulse, with a drizzle of some of the dulse butter from the
parcel pan over the top.

Crab linguine

Serves 4 (you should get enough out of one crab for this)

400g linguine pasta (or try it with fresh sea spaghetti)

a good glug of olive oil

2 garlic cloves, finely chopped

½ tsp chilli flakes

100ml white wine

200g brown crab meat

salt

a squeeze of lemon (save a few wedges, to serve)

a small bunch parsley, finely chopped to make about 2 heaped tbsp

200g white crab meat (the bigger the pieces, the better)

One of the simplest and best crab (or pasta, for that matter) dishes going. Ever popular on the menu and a real showcase for luxurious but fuss-free food. Assuming the crab meat has been prepared, it's on the table in minutes.

For an interesting – and gluten free – alternative, the pasta can be replaced with sea spaghetti. Just gently blanch some and use it in place of the pasta.

If your crab still needs to be picked, refer to the instructions on pages 87–89. Gather all the ingredients (it's best to do this all at once) and boil the pasta.

Heat a really good glug of olive oil in a pan big enough to take everything. Once at a medium heat, add the garlic and chilli flakes and let them cook for a minute, stirring constantly.

Increase to a high heat and add the wine, moving it around a bit and letting it simmer for a few minutes – until it eventually merges with the oil.

Add the brown meat and a good pinch of salt, then turn down the heat to medium again. Combine with the wine/oil to form a rough sauce.

When it's ready, use tongs to add the linguine to the pan, tossing it around to really incorporate the sauce into it.

Add the squeeze of lemon, the parsley (reserving a little for garnish) and the white meat, and carefully mix, trying not to break the meat up too much.

Divide between wide bowls and add a final sprinkle of parsley and a wedge of lemon.

Whole lobster

Like crab, the luxurious simplicity of a whole lobster, fresh from the sea, cooked well, with as little done to it as possible, is nigh on unbeatable. We serve lobsters whole with sides, or as part of a platter along with a whole crab, some langoustine and whatever else the red man and Craig come across that day. I guess it's no surprise that often it's the lobster that is chosen as the star of the dish.

There are many ways to cook a lobster, and I have to admit that when I took on the restaurant I had previously only cooked them for myself and my family. Canna is owned by the National Trust for Scotland and the very first diners I ever had were a party of their most important donors – all of whom wanted lobster, of course. I phoned my mate Steve, who runs a hotel and seafood restaurant. His chef talked me through these steps on the phone and it's been our tried-and-tested method ever since.

The sides are the same as for the whole crab – a good mayo or aioli, some salad (you need something to counteract the richness) and some good bread. Here we also give the option of smoked dulse butter – it offers a meaty, bacony taste that complements the lobster well. A squeeze of lemon is most definitely a worthy alternative, however.

If using, make the butter first. Smoke the dulse by either placing it in a freezer bag and injecting smoke into it with a smoking gun, then seal; otherwise, place the dulse on a tray and put it in a lit BBQ with a scattering of wood chips. Leave it as long as possible (at least an hour).

Combine the dulse flakes and salt in a large bowl, cut the butter into two chunks and roll in the butter to thoroughly coat in dulse.

Next, with your lobster prepped, get a roasting tray and loosely line the bottom with greaseproof paper. Heat the oven to 210°C.

1 lobster per person

1 lobster, prepped as per p. 90

1 tbsp smoked dulse butter, if using

a wedge of lemon, to serve

For the smoked dulse butter

2 tbsp dulse flakes (for directions see p. 31)

1 tsp sea salt

50g really good-quality unsalted butter

Half the lobster, continuing on from the prepping instructions on page 90. Starting at the front, but this time going towards the back, continue the incision already made, cutting the head in half lengthways. When you get to the tail, it's best to push the knife down and through the first section, then, keeping the point on the chopping board, lever down to do the rest in a oner.

With the lobster completely in two, twist off the legs and place the two halves, flesh side down, on the roasting tray. Crack each of the claws with the back of a knife – you just want to create a split, not break the shell off, then add them to the tray too.

Roast for 10–12 minutes or until it just transitions from black to red.

To serve, place a knob of the smoked dulse butter on the flesh and serve with your choice of accompaniments.

Langoustine – as they are

This is hardly a recipe – all you need is langoustine, that's it! – but it's the biggest bang for your cooking buck possible. It's the easiest and fastest way to make an incredible plate of food. Delicious to munch through and a fun, sociable sharer, these gorgeous creatures are fantastic. All you need is a pot – and access to fresh, live langoustine.

If you want to peel them like a pro, see page 94.

Add the usual culprits – home-made bread, a good salad and some mayo or aioli – for a simple shellfish feast.

I suggest you serve
7–10 medium langoustine
per person

In a large pan, add enough water to cover the langoustine and get it up to a rolling boil. Add a lot of salt (seawater is great for this, if you're happy with it; that gives you an idea of the salinity we're after).

Drop in the langoustine. As soon as the pan returns to a boil, they are ready – 3–5 minutes.

Drain or remove immediately, then either eat them or place them in cold water to halt the cooking process.

Serve with a wedge of lemon and your choice of accompaniment.

Langoustine and smoked haddock pie

Makes 5–6 pies
(our tins measure 11.5 x 3.5cm)

For the pastry

290g soft butter

650g plain flour

½ tsp salt

130ml water

For the mash

1kg floury potatoes
(e.g. Maris Piper or
King Edward)

50g butter

25ml milk

For the stock

langoustine shells
(left from the filling)

½ onion (leave skin on and
no need to chop)

1 celery stick, roughly
chopped

1 carrot, roughly chopped
(no need to peel)

1 tbsp tomato puree

1 bay leaf

Everybody loves a fish pie! This is our version.

We pared it down to our favourite parts of the filling – the smoked haddock and the prawns (and replaced these with plump local langoustine). We have a smokery nearby that does incredible peat-smoked fish – their haddock is gorgeous.

It's optional, but if you've read the rest of this book you'll know that we believe in a pie that has pastry sides and bottom. And we see no reason why fish pies shouldn't either. You can make the pastry and the stock the day before.

To make the pastry, in a food mixer (or with your hands) combine the butter, flour and salt. If the butter is not easily malleable, microwave for 20 seconds at a time until it is. If it melts completely, the recipe will work just fine. Mix until very rough breadcrumbs have formed – if using your hands, rub the flour into the butter between thumb and fingers.

Pour in half the water and continue to mix, then add the rest. At this point it should have come together into a robust dough that would hold its shape if cut in half. If too wet, add more flour and mix; if too dry, a touch more water.

Remove from the bowl/machine and knead for a minute or two on a clean surface. Once it has come together into a smooth ball, you can use it directly, but it is preferable to wrap it in cling film and place it in the fridge for 30 minutes to an hour (or up to two days). If the dough becomes too hard when cold, microwave it quickly before use.

Next, create the mash. Peel and cut the potatoes into chunks, then boil them until soft but not falling apart. Whilst cooking, heat the butter and milk. Drain the potatoes and either pass them through a ricer (this is best) or mash them – then add the heated butter/milk and mix thoroughly.

CAFÉ CA
RESTAURAN
HACIENDA
GRIÑÓN
Open

Cook the langoustine in boiling water and peel (see p. 94, for step-by-step instructions), reserving one whole for each pie for garnish.

Use the water they were cooked in, as well as the shells, to make the stock. Place the langoustine shells in a pan and just covering with the reserved water. Add the other stock ingredients and simmer for an hour, then strain.

To make the filling, melt the butter in a large pan, then stir in the flour and continue to cook for 2–3 minutes. Gradually stir in the stock, then add the wine and finely chopped stalks of the parsley. Simmer for 20 minutes. Remove from the heat and add the cream, chopped parsley leaves, anchovies, haddock and seasoning. Reserve the langoustine for the next step.

To assemble the pie, line the pie tins with greaseproof paper and pastry in exactly the same way as the beef pie (see p. 178). As these pies will have a mash rather than a pastry top, neatly cut around the top of the tin for a smooth, circular top.

Half fill each with the fish mixture, then divide the langoustine between the pies, laying more fish sauce on top.

Heap a pile of mash on top of each pie, going right to the edge. Optionally, create a hole down through the middle of the pie and place a reserved langoustine in it, so that it appears to be bursting out of the top.

Bake for 30–40 minutes until the mash is starting to go golden. Serve with a simple side of veg.

Laurel delivering the rioja blanco

For the filling

50g butter

50g plain flour

500ml langoustine stock

100ml white wine

small bunch of parsley

200ml double cream

2 anchovies, finely chopped

250g fresh haddock in large bite-size chunks

250g smoked haddock in large bite-size chunks

salt and freshly ground black pepper

1–1.2kg whole langoustine

Spice-roasted whole mackerel

Serves 4

4 large whole mackerel, gutted but with heads still on (see p. 83 for step-by-step instructions)

1 tbsp coriander

1 tbsp cumin

1 tbsp garlic powder

1 tsp ground ginger

2 tbsp paprika

2 tbsp tomato paste

2 tsp salt

40ml olive oil

Roasting mackerel is one of our favourite ways to cook it: so simple, and the natural oiliness of the fish means it will stay juicy. This dish is one for when we have an abundance. In June and July we get absolute whoppers – going way off the plate on both sides, roasted to just cooked on the inside, with a crispy skin and the spiced marinade permeating through. This is a great way to eat. We serve this with either bread (see p. 213) or chips and a simple salad (see p. 220).

Score the mackerel diagonally 3 times on each side. Combine all of the other ingredients into a paste and rub into the mackerel, ensuring the scores are well filled.

You can cook it immediately, but it's better to refrigerate for a few hours to let the flavours do their thing.

Preheat the oven to 210°C and roast the mackerel for 15–20 minutes, depending on the size of the fish.

Smoked paprika and garlic mackerel, with crispy dulse

Mackerel works really well with the smoky tang of paprika – simply roast with lemon and garlic, and this is an incredibly quick and fresh way to cook the fillets. Lovely with salad or just boiled potatoes, or we serve it with our rhubarb, cannellini bean and potato bake (see p. 219), which is sticky, delicious and well worth the few extra minutes of prep.

Serves 4

8 mackerel fillets (see p. 83. for prep instructions)

2–3 tsp smoked paprika

2 garlic cloves, finely chopped

olive oil

1 handful of dried dulse (optional)

wedge of lemon, to serve

———————

Oil a baking sheet and place the mackerel fillets skin side down, then sprinkle with smoked paprika, garlic and a glug of olive oil.

To make the crispy dulse, rub the olive oil into the seaweed and place on the tray too – try and leave some space between it and the mackerel. Roast for 10 minutes.

Plate up the fillets and finish with the crispy dulse and a wedge of lemon.

Lobster, crab and langoustine lasagne

Serves 4

For the stock

the shells from the lobster and langoustine used in the sauce

2 carrots, not peeled, just chopped in half

1 celery stick, roughly chopped

2 tbsp tomato puree

1 bay leaf

10 whole peppercorns

2 tsp salt

For the sauce

50g butter

1 onion, finely chopped

1 carrot, diced

½ bulb fennel, finely chopped

1 celery stick, finely chopped

20 fennel seeds

300ml white wine

75ml white wine vinegar

1 tbsp tomato puree

1 x 400g tin tomatoes

1 litre stock (use the shells as per the stock instructions, or you could make crab stock (see p. 150))

500ml double cream

a pinch of cayenne pepper

1 tsp (or more, to taste) salt

squeeze of lemon juice

There is an old school seafood restaurant called Wheelers in Kent. It's a real inspiration and, if you can get yourself a table, an incredible place to enjoy classic, simple produce done well in a 'time stood still' setting. Their signature dish is lobster lasagne, and this recipe is very loosely based on it. It is light, lobstery and luscious. To beef it up a bit, we use actual pasta for the layers (they use wonton wrappers) and have added langoustine – useful for both making the stock and adding further meatiness. Even with some further simplifications, it is a time-consuming and 'all of the pans' type of dish, but the result is utter decadence.

First, prepare, cook and extract the meat from the lobster (p. 90), langoustine (p. 94) and crab (p. 87).

Make the stock. The crab stock (as per the bisque recipe – see p. 150) is amazing for this, if you happen to have some. Otherwise, roast the shells you retained after preparing and cooking the langoustine and the lobster in the oven at 210°C for 10 minutes, then transfer to a pot with the rest of the stock ingredients, cover with water, then simmer slowly for an hour. Drain through a sieve and set to one side. You'll use this for the sauce.

To make the sauce, begin by melting the butter in a pan and frying the onion, carrot, fennel, celery and fennel seeds until soft (around 10 minutes). Increase the heat and add the wine and vinegar, then reduce back down, so you've almost the same amount of liquid as before they were added.

Add the puree, tomatoes and stock, and cook until reduced by about half. Add the cream, cayenne, salt and lemon, and continue to heat until thickened.

For the crab filling, fry the leek in the butter and season. When soft, add the cream, parmesan, lemon juice, cayenne and crab meat, and season with salt and pepper.

Next prepare the mushroom filling. Fry the shallot, garlic and mushrooms in butter until softened, then remove from the heat and sprinkle with parsley.

Once all the elements are prepared, bring a pan of salted water to the boil and cook the pasta until it is al dente.

When you are ready to assemble the dish, place a cooked lasagne sheet on the plate and top with the crab filling, then the lobster pieces. Add another lasagne sheet on top, then layer it with the mushrooms and the langoustine. Add another sheet and the sauce, then finish with the parmesan.

For the crab filling

20g butter

1 leek, finely chopped

1 tbsp double cream

20g parmesan, finely grated

juice of ½ lemon

a pinch of cayenne pepper

100g white crab meat
(you'll get a lot more than this from one crab - you can either add more or use for something else)

salt and freshly ground black pepper

For the mushroom filling

1 tbsp butter

½ shallot, finely chopped

½ garlic clove, finely chopped

100g chestnut mushrooms

2 tbsp parsley, finely chopped

To assemble

12 lasagne sheets

2 large lobsters, prepared and cooked (retain shells for stock), cut into large slices

500g langoustine, prepared and cooked (retain shells for stock)

4 tbsp parmesan, finely grated

Home-smoked mackerel

Each fillet serves 1 person,
for a light lunch

mackerel, filleted (see p. 83 for
step-by-step instructions): feel
free to use however many you
want or however many will fit
on your tray

1–2 tsp salt per fillet pair

3 tbsp tea leaves per tray

2 tbsp wood chippings,
e.g. pine or apple wood,
per tray

1 tbsp rice per tray

Mackerel arrive by the bucketload in summer and smoking them
yourself is a great way to cook this fine fish, using a time-honoured
method of preservation. This lovely recipe makes a simple, healthy
stand-out lunch from a delicious ingredient.

You can also use the resulting smoked mackerel to make the
croquettes (p. 47) or, for lunch, serve it as it is with the potato and
wild mint salad (p. 208) and some nice home-made bread (p. 213).

For this, you will need a roasting tray with a rack that will sit
inside.

———————

Once you have filleted your mackerel, rub salt generously into the fish
and leave for 30 minutes before rinsing off with cold water. Pat dry.

Scatter the tea leaves, wood chippings and rice into the roasting tray
and place the rack on top. Ensure the rack is suspended above and
not touching the leaves/chippings.

Place the mackerel on the rack, then cover and seal well with kitchen
foil. Place this over a medium hob for 10 minutes.

Check the fillet is cooked through, then either eat immediately with
crusty bread and salad, or refrigerate for up to 3 days.

Pan-fried mackerel sandwich with tartare sauce

A king of sandwiches! When the mackerel are around, fresh from the sea, this is a seriously gorgeous sarny – the hot oily fish and crispy skin balanced perfectly with the tartare sauce.

Tartare is one of those condiments that, when home-made, is incomparable to shop-bought. It's incredibly easy to put together, too. The exact quantities are up to you – we make this constantly at the restaurant and it's slightly different, but always delicious, every time.

———————

Prepare the tartare. Put all the ingredients, except the mayo, in a bowl and mix thoroughly. Add the mayo a spoon at a time and mix until you're happy with the consistency – mixing as you go is important; you need a lot less mayo than you'd imagine.

For the fish, melt some butter in a frying pan on a high heat and fry the fillets skin side down until the skin has crisped (try not to move them until this has happened; it will stop the skin from tearing off). Flip the fillets and fry for a further minute, then turn the heat off.

Butter the bread and add 2 fillets per sandwich. Dollop tartare on top. Enjoy!

Serves 2

4 large mackerel fillets (or more if you like/they are small)

butter, for frying, and some for spreading

home-made bread (see p. 213)

home-made tartare (see below)

For the tartare sauce

small bunch of parsley (maybe 75g), finely chopped

a handful of gherkins, finely chopped

1 shallot, finely chopped

2 tbsp capers

2 tbsp white wine vinegar

1 tsp salt

good (or home-made) mayonnaise

Crab bisque

Makes enough for 2–3 bowls
(about a litre)

For the stock

2 crabs worth of shells, following
the removal of all the meat –
body, legs, all broken shell, the
head (minus the 'face' and sack
behind, and the dead man's
fingers)

110ml white wine

1 large onion, halved
(leave the skin on)

2 carrots, roughly chopped
(no need to peel)

1 stick celery, roughly chopped

2 tbsp tomato paste

2 sprigs of thyme
(or 1 tbsp dried)

1 bay leaf

10–15 whole peppercorns

1–2 tsp salt

To finish the bisque

2 tbsp unsalted butter

4 shallots, chopped
(or one onion)

150ml white wine

50g white rice

2 tbsp tomato paste

½ tsp salt

¼ tsp cayenne pepper

200ml double cream

Bisque, in the traditional form, is a soup made only from seafood shells. It is an absolute luxury created out of something that is often thrown away. In our kitchen, making this soup is basically considered the final step in the crab meat-picking process. The recipe is the result of years of doing this: it is quick, rustic and incredibly flavourful. The ingredients are highly negotiable – we often swap wine for brandy, or carrot for another sweet vegetable (red cabbage, say). If you don't have exactly what is below, don't be afraid to experiment. Rich and delicious all by itself, we also use it as a sauce for our ravioli (p. 101).

———————

First, make the stock. This forms the basis of the bisque but has many alternative uses (and freezes very well, if you want to finish the soup some other time). Place all the crab shells on a tray and roast for 30 minutes at 160°C (this is an optional step but increases the flavour).

Add the roasted shells to a large pot and with a rolling pin bash them up a bit to condense them and open up the bodies.

Add water to about an inch over the shells and bring to a simmer (do not boil). Cover and leave on the lowest heat for an hour.

Add all of the stock ingredients – it will be sieved out at the end, so the vegetables can be very roughly chopped. Increase the heat slightly and simmer for another 30 minutes. Sieve into a container and set aside.

To make the bisque, give the pot a rinse and place it back on the heat. Soften the shallots in the butter for 10 minutes. Add the stock, wine, rice and tomato paste, and bring to a simmer, then cover for 30 minutes. Take off the heat and blend with a hand blender.

Finally, stir in the salt, cayenne and, according to taste, the cream (if you prefer a more pungent bisque, consider using less).

THE LAND

Wildflowers, Fruit, Vegetables and Meat

The beating heart of Canna's soil is the farm and it's been so for centuries: the varied and spectacular fields and wild grazing; and on parts that aren't managed now, the raised beds of crofters from a past age are still evident. The meat that we're lucky enough to use can be found all around the restaurant and in every nook and cranny beyond.

The fertile land supports numerous and varied options for foraging, too. Wild plants and flowers grow all over our hedgerows, hills and meadows, along the shoreline and in the woods. It's hard to imagine a more pleasant and compact land to peruse: wild garlic carpets the floor of the trees behind the restaurant in spring, wild gorse lights up the valleys when in bloom. There are umpteen species that we haven't even featured here – pig nuts and pine, pineapple weed and sea arrowgrass (a sort of wild coriander – it's amazing!). We have focused on what might be found most elsewhere and the fine ingredients we use most often in the kitchen.

No less exciting are the vegetables, organically grown right over our wall in the grounds of Canna House, where the friut comes from too – strawberries, blackcurrants and gooseberries, and an orchard of apples and pears.

We're still waiting for the first olive from the tree planted many years ago – and may be waiting some time longer – but the fertile land, and the use of seaweed to mulch and fertilise (it's nutrient rich – is there anything seaweed can't do?!), produces a fabulous crop of giant vegetables and beautiful garnishes that are a joy to cook with.

Pete doesn't just play the tunes - here he is tending to the orchard behind the restaurant

Wildflowers, Fruit and Vegetables

It's a huge effort to nurture food from the soil and, whilst we make a community day out of gathering seaweed from the shore and slathering the plots with it, and many help in all sorts of ways, it has to be said that Liz – oracle of mushroom knowledge and master organic vegetable grower – is in charge. The veg gets used by us, but is also offered to the community. It's a very special contribution to the island.

When it comes to foraging on the land, it's a little different from seaweed in some obvious (and less obvious) ways. Wellies are unlikely to fill with water – a welcome bonus. There is safety for the beginner with seaweed however, as there are no poisonous varieties in the UK. Not so with land vegetables. To warn through example, hogweed is a delicious wild plant. Giant hogweed is similar looking but highly poisonous, and hemlock water dropwort is also similar but one of the most poisonous in the UK – and it was this that I fried up with some butter, having incorrectly identified it as hogweed. I lived, but lesson learned. I was very lucky – it could have easily been a different story. Be very careful and do not eat something unless you have identified it carefully. Speak to somebody around who knows (I told Liz about the hemlock afterwards and she just about slapped her plant bible across my head).

beetroot

Gorse

Gorse is abundant in Scotland. You'll see it in all regions. There's certainly plenty of it here on the west coast. It's a big, brown, bushy, prickly – very prickly (horribly prickly) – shrub awash with small yellow flowers. Unusually the flowers can be seen in any season: 'When gorse is out of bloom, kissing is out of season', as the saying goes. Mid to late spring is the best time for it – when the flowers really take it over.

You'll often smell it before you see it, and what an aroma. Coconut and sweet, it doesn't seem to belong in Scotland. It reminds me of suntan lotion and holidays.

Pick it in full bloom and note that flowers can taste different depending on whether they face the sun or not. Try it – those facing the sun will be sweeter and more coconut-like; those facing away are a bit more savoury, like a fresh pea from a pod perhaps. If you notice a difference, go for the former, otherwise I guess it doesn't matter.

Picking is not a quick win. Most people advise doing so by hand, even if that means getting prickled a lot (they're fiddly). My tip is to use silicon-ended tongs – there's a knack to it, but you can slide the tongs over the flowers and, using the right amount of pressure, the flowers will come away but not the needles/buds.

To do anything with it, you need A LOT. We usually make a gorse syrup – the best way to store this flower. From it you can make all kinds of things – cocktails, cordials, ice creams. For one litre of syrup, you need about half a kilo of flowers. It might not sound much, but it's a large freezer bag packed with them.

Diluted, the syrup makes a lovely summer cordial or can be used as an enhancer to a gin and tonic. Obviously it lends itself to being a flavour in many types of dessert – I think it works best in creamy types. You can add it to a standard ice-cream recipe, say, or try one of our most popular desserts, our gorse-flower crème brûlée (p. 237).

Gorse syrup

Add the water and sugar to a pan and bring it to the boil. Simmer for 10 minutes, then remove from the heat. Add the gorse flowers, and the lemon and orange zest and juice. Mix together, pushing the flowers down to fully submerge them. Infuse for 12–24 hours. Heat the mixture until the syrup liquifies, then strain it all through a muslin (or tea towel). You can either use it immediately or, if you are intending to store it, carefully pour the syrup into sterilised jars or bottles and seal. To sterilise the jars, fill a pan with water, submerge the jars, bring the water to a boil for 3 minutes, then air dry.

1.5 litres water

750g sugar

750g gorse flowers (approx. 1–2 235 x 380ml freezer bags – flowers only, no twigs, spikes, etc.)

1 lemon, zest and juice

1 orange, zest and juice

Wild garlic

Wild garlic – like butter, cheese, salt and its more inhibited brother, normal garlic – is one of those ingredients that will improve almost any savoury dish. It also makes a great garnish and I hear it's very good for you too (having antibacterial and antiseptic, as well as blood pressure-reducing, qualities).

For the forager, it's an easy one to find. Too easy, perhaps. Not that it's a competition, but on Canna, like many places, the woodland floor is absolutely carpeted in swathes of it. Appearing at a time of year that is otherwise quite sparse (and when we could most do with some healthy greenery), its timing is impeccable.

The short harvesting season begins around mid-March. When the flowers appear on the plant, about a month or two later, the oomph has begun to wane.

The blankets of thick, grassy leaves are fairly obvious. Identification is straightforward – it smells of garlic, and tastes of garlic. Just stick to harvesting the leaf and snip it away rather than dislodging the whole plant. Be nice and avoid decimating an area – you don't need much.

Wild garlic freezes very well. But I'd do it immediately after picking. It will lose its lush appearance once it's defrosted, but the taste certainly lasts, so it's great in cooked dishes. Place rinsed leaves loosely in freezer bags and tie, allowing air to remain so they can be shaken.

Wild garlic is a great side dish – simply steam it for a minute or two and plate it up – or can be used as a straight swap for garlic in recipes. When fresh coriander is not available, we shred wild garlic as a garnish for curries. The flowers make a great touch to any dish once they're in bloom.

Wild garlic oil

Making oil is a fantastic way to preserve wild garlic's goodness, but it is also a very versatile option in itself. Drizzled over salad, it is amazing, or you can use it to create a luscious garlic mayonnaise, say. We use it in our moules marinière dish. Once made, it will last for a week if sealed and kept in the fridge. It freezes very well, though, too. This recipe makes 400ml. You only need drops of it in most dishes, so this will provide plenty.

400g wild garlic, leaves only

400g good olive oil

First, wash the wild garlic leaves to remove any dirt. Bring a pan of water to the boil and add the wild garlic for 1–2 minutes. Drain into a colander and stop the cooking by running under a cold tap until no longer warm throughout. Add the leaves to a food processor or blender and whizz for a few minutes before adding oil 100ml at a time. Pass through a sieve, then it's ready to use or store.

Mint

Around from spring until winter, mint grows rapidly and – if you can find yourself a patch – is a reliable provider. The plants grow up to around one metre in height, are hairy-leaved with a square stem, and the leaves are arranged in alternating opposites. But obviously its minty-ness is the real identifier, both in smell and taste. You'll find it all over the shop (not literally) in woodland and hedgerows. It grows a lot by the side of the road on Canna.

Just gather the leaves and wash them thoroughly. I'd encourage more use of mint in cooking – it makes the difference between an 'all right' and a 'great' potato salad. It also adds fresh zing to salads and Asian dishes. Also perfect for a simple cup of tea – just pop the leaves in and add boiling water.

Mint can be dried (see dehydration, pp. 26–27) and frozen (although they obviously won't look quite as fresh after thawing – but the taste is there).

We're lucky to have this growing right beside the restaurant

Wild thyme

One of the handiest wild herbs, thyme can be found growing in dense carpets throughout the UK and is one of the more obviously useful finds for the forager. You can use it directly instead of cultivated thyme, so it is brilliant in many soups and stews. It goes particularly well with red meat.

In summer, it flowers and the thick green carpets become punctuated with pink/purple little petals (a great garnish). It often grows low down, on grassy banks and rocky outcrops – you can find it along the road in many places on Canna. The plant itself is woody-stemmed, with small oval leaves. It is obvious to the nose if you pick and rub some.

Any recipe that uses thyme can make use of the wild variety. I often find myself mid-recipe, disappearing to walk down the road, eyes on the side looking for some. We also make a refreshing ice cream out of it and wild mint (p. 238) that pairs really well with rich desserts.

Nettles

Foraging in the woods
behind the restaurant

Nettles, for me and my mates – and I'm sure many others – gave us our first understanding that wild plants have uses. If you got stung, you sought out dock leaves to 'cure' them. The science, I believe, is in some doubt, but the lesson remains all the same, I think.

Beyond opening children's minds to the medicinal use of plants, nettles are well known to the forager's kitchen. Abundant and easy to gather, it has some fantastic sweet and savoury applications – one of the best is the ubiquitous soup! At Café Canna, we like to use it in our spanakopita (p. 206).

When it starts to appear in early spring, nettles are a tasty and nutritious option. You can pick them later in the year, but it's always best to collect the newer, smaller growth than the tough and haggard older growth. Once they have flowers, they tend to be past it.

Wear gloves and cover your arms. Nettle stings used to seem like death was around the corner, but they're really not that bad.

Meat

Despite having the farm all around us, this was the last piece of the jigsaw in trying to source everything from our local environment. Cows and sheep need to be processed and tracked in ways that legally make it very difficult to use from the island. Happily, we've since found a way and are lucky enough to be using Canna-bred meat across the menus – and unbelievably gorgeous stuff it is, too.

It is well documented that happy animals make the best meat – and it is actually fairly obvious to see that our cattle are just that. The ground is lush and the grazing varied – I'm not sure if cattle appreciate views, but if they do, these guys have it made. They're looked over by farmers who really care and the end result is extremely high-quality meat, raised with the highest welfare standards.

Beyond the farm, Canna has very few wild game options. Any venison we have on the menu comes from neighbouring Rum or other local areas. We do have rabbits, though – and these have been part of many Café Canna menus.

Rabbit

Canna, like many remote areas of Scotland, has its fair share of rabbits. Here, their famously care-free approach to reproduction has been supplemented by a couple of factors. First, it's probably just a bloody brilliant place to be a rabbit. Other than the eagles and the rabbit man, there are no predators. The landscape looks like it's been designed for them. Perhaps most importantly, myxomatosis was never a thing here. In 2008, a successful attempt to rid Canna of its rat population handed the humble bunny the keys to the island.

The intervention was a good thing – and it worked. The decimated rare bird populations started to grow again, and we now enjoy a rat-free island (they are a real issue on some others). However, the rabbit

The rabbit man
with the catch

population became so large that it was causing considerable problems – so many burrows that entire roads and sides of hills were collapsing. So now the numbers are held in check by our resident rabbit man. I guess over the years our diners have done their bit, too.

Rabbit is a fantastic meat – scandalously under-appreciated. Being a wild game, it is incredibly lean, healthy and nutritious. It is also tasty in a not too gamey kind of way – very accessible. For the cook, wild rabbit takes some getting used to and is one of the more challenging meats to cook well – it can easily be made tough or dry. The first attempt we made heralded some surprises, that's for sure. The best advice is a common one – either cook it very quickly, or for an age. Long and slow – use cooking times as vague opinion and keep going until tender.

The leftovers from any butchery make a fantastic stock. Chuck them in a pan and cover with water. Add some veg – a whole onion and some peppercorns perhaps, and some sweetness, a carrot and some cabbage, if you like. I'd also add a magazine-sized bit of kelp. Simmer for 4 to 5 hours.

If you're buying rabbit from a butcher, there is a good chance the rabbit will be farmed. If it looks surprisingly big for a bunny, it is almost certain to be. This is fine – you may just reduce cooking time, as farmed rabbit is not as tough, that's all.

Confit – as we use it in the cassoulet recipe (p. 190) – is an ideal way to cook rabbit, partly because it's so easy but also because, even with wild rabbit, it's sure to be moist. Confit rabbit makes delicious croquettes (just mix it with some béchamel and coat in breadcrumbs – use it in place of mackerel, say; see p. 47). We've been known to use it as a sandwich filling (Coronation rabbit is very popular). Stewed or à la moutarde are the classics and well worth a go, as is a pie – an interesting centrepiece for everyone to tuck into. Our favourite is rabbit stew (p. 193), while rabbit sausage rolls always go quickly (p. 201).

How to joint a rabbit

You need a big, sturdy knife or cleaver for this. You also may need to put a decent amount of strength/weight on the blade – so if you're uncomfortable with this, a safer option is to place the blade, then tap the top of it with a rolling pin or something else, rather than manhandling it through.

We'll assume the rabbit is skinned already – if not, get wherever you got it from to do it. If there are kidneys and liver in the cavity, it's best to remove these first to get them out the way (they normally just pull away). Set them aside and use with the rest of the meat – they are delicious.

1. Remove the front legs. Take each individually, twist it so that the shoulder-blade sticks out. Cut behind that so the blade comes away with as much peripheral meat as possible.

2. For the hind legs, you need to cut through the socket. Getting this right makes it surprisingly easy. If you're struggling to cut through, you haven't got things lined up. Starting at the front of the leg, cut through the top of the thigh following the line of the body. Do the same from the back. This line should generally lead you directly to the socket, where you can finish the removal of the leg with a firm bit of weight on the blade through the middle of it. There's usually a flap of skin (the belly flap) on each side, running from the rib cage to the rear. Remove this, it's lovely – just bung it in with the meat.

3. Remove the rib cage. You're going to remove it from about the second rib up, so make an incision between the second and third rib on each side.

4. Turn it over and find a gap in the spine that matches up with the incisions and cut through the back bone to remove the rear loin-less section, too.

5. All that should be left now is the central back bone with the prized loin running up it. Chop this into two, three or even four, if particularly large (you want each piece to be 3cm to 4cm).

6. A jointed rabbit, with the loin and legs ready for the pot, and the ribcage and hind area for stock

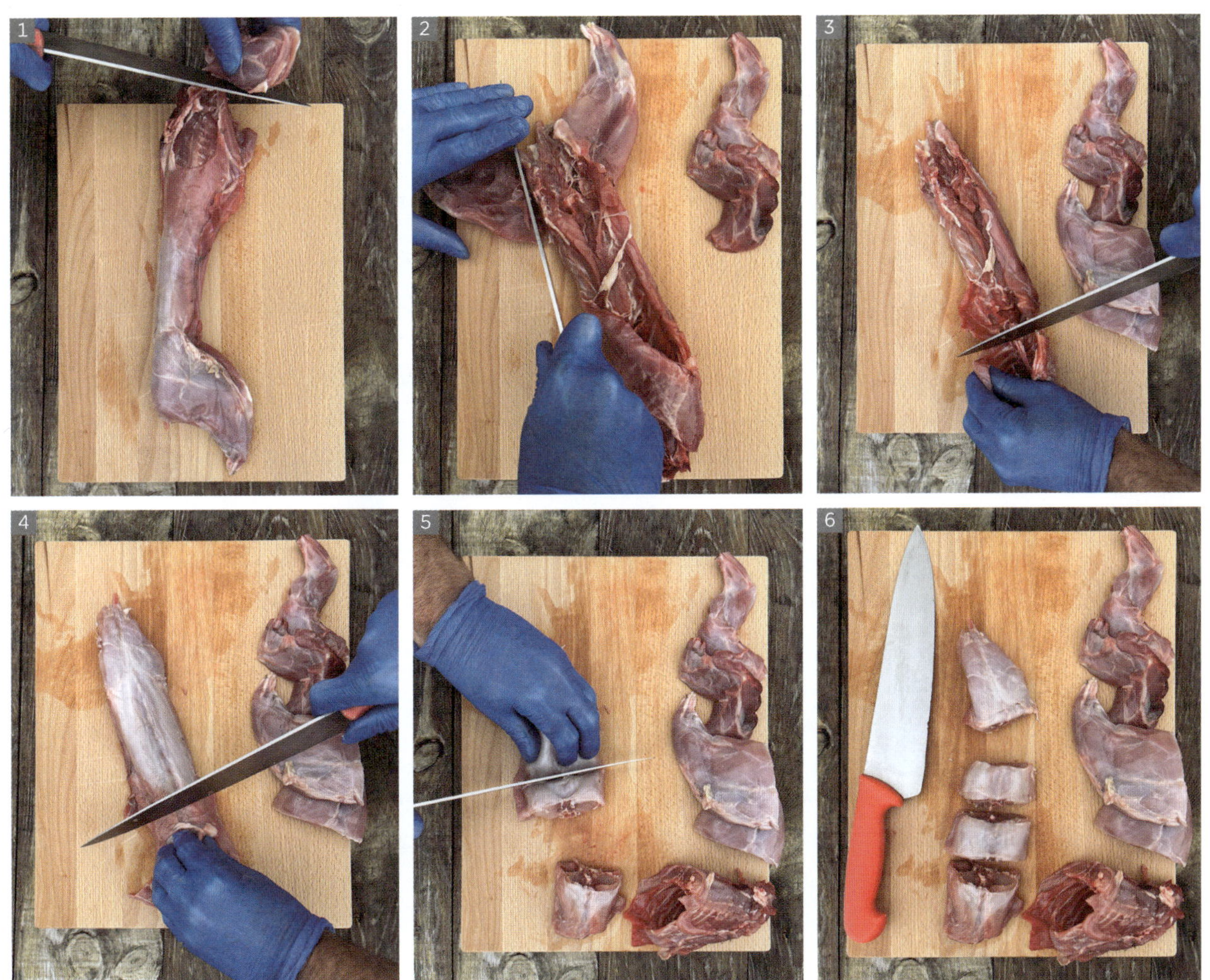

Beef

Gerry, Caroline and
Booger the Beltie

Our beef comes from the locally raised Belted Galloways (named because their coats look like they have a white belt around them). It's a hardy breed that is becoming increasingly recognised as producers of some of the finest beef in the country. They mature comparatively slowly and have particularly thick skin (sounds like my school report card), which creates a well-marbled, very flavourful, tender and juicy meat. You'll see them mooing about in the fields surrounding the restaurant. They're lovely animals, and are raised with respect, skill and love, and that is obvious in the end product.

Beef and Blue Murder (a blue cheese from Tain) is one of our most popular dishes – a large (some say too large, but I don't listen) pie rammed with Beltie beef in a rich ale sauce (p. 177). We love a roast beef, a home salted and a steak sandwich (with garlic mayo and pickles, it is an amazing lunch), or pulled beef could be used really well as a replacement for dulse or mackerel in the croquettes (p. 47).

Mutton

It was Murdo – farmer, coastguard, fixer of potholes and so many other things (we named our beer after him – 'the Jack', as in Murdo Jack) – who got me into mutton. Before living on the island, I can't remember ever having it before.

Murdo has the diet of a king – it consists entirely of only three things: lobster, mutton and cauliflower cheese. He's bang on about all of them, of course, but mutton was an unexpected surprise to me. How something so tasty can get such a bad name, I do not understand. Juicy, tender and flavourful, lamb is a poor man's mutton, make no mistake about it.

The chops are a good first bet – best simply seasoned and fried in butter. Mutton is also excellent for curry – we do it Caribbean style, in place of the usual goat (p. 188). If you are making an Indian curry, mutton is way better than lamb. Mutton dhansak is a proper stunner. Another favourite is a sort of Canna-style cassoulet – with mutton, venison sausages and rabbit in place of the usual ingredients (p. 190).

Murdo and the mutton

RECIPES FROM THE LAND

Beef, Skye Black ale and Blue Murder pie

Pea and wild garlic risotto

Butter rabbit curry

Masala-spiced cauliflower cheese pie

Curry mutton

Canna cassoulet

Rabbit stew

Beef (and dulse skirlie) olives

Mutton shanks

Beetroot and mushroom bourguignon

Rabbit and chutney sausage roll

Wild garlic and brie pasty

Isle of Mull cheddar macaroni pies

Nettle and spinach spanakopita

Potato and wild mint salad

Pea and wild mint soup

Beef, Skye Black ale and Blue Murder pie

You should cook what you love, and so there is no question that pies will always be on our menu. Fully encased in golden shortcrust, bursting with meaty, oozy filling, they are a simple and rewarding culinary addiction.

We're very proud of the locally reared beef that we use for these – raised on the hills around us, the animals' happy, free, natural life is very evident in the taste. The meat is slow-cooked in Skye Black, a rich, dark ale brewed just across the water, to create a thick and flavourful stew. Blue Murder – a Scottish blue cheese – adds a further creamy layer to the filling, and we serve all this with a silky wholegrain mustard mash (p. 225), some vegetables from the plot (p. 223), and yet more gravy.

Shortcrust pastry is very easy to make. There is no dark art, you do not need cold hands – the method below is simple, quick and can be completely relied upon.

Make the filling by first sweating the onions for at least 10 minutes until soft and very slightly coloured in a pot large enough to hold all the ingredients. Add the mustard and 1½ tablespoons of flour and mix to form a thick paste. Continue to cook for 5 minutes, then turn off the heat.

Working in batches, dust the beef with the seasoned flour and fry quickly in a very hot, well-oiled pan until browned. As each batch is done (it should only take a minute), place it into the pot with the onion.

Once all the meat has been browned, deglaze the pan with a little of the beer and pour/scrape all of that into the onion pot too.

Add the carrots, ale, bay leaves, thyme, Worcester sauce and salt, and then pour in the stock to a few centimetres above the meat.

Makes 7 pies
(using 11.5 x 3.5cm tins)

For the pastry

290g soft butter

650g plain flour

½ tsp salt

130ml water

For the filling

2 onions, chopped

2 tsp Dijon mustard

1½ heaped tbsp plain flour

8 tbsp seasoned plain flour
(for dusting)

800g beef (shoulder, brisket –
any stewing-style cut), cut into
sizeable chunks

2 large carrots, cubed

500ml stout/ale

2 bay leaves

2 tsp thyme

2 tbsp Worcester sauce

1 tsp salt

300ml beef stock

175g Blue Murder cheese
(or any blue cheese)

1 egg, beaten

Partially cover and simmer until the meat is tender (approximately 2 hours). Check occasionally, and towards the end, if there appears to be excess liquid, remove the lid completely.

Whilst the beef is cooking, make the pastry. In a food mixer (or with your hands), combine the butter, flour and salt. If the butter is not easily malleable, microwave for 20 seconds at a time until it is. If it melts completely, the recipe will work just fine. Mix until very rough breadcrumbs have formed – if using your hands, rub the flour into the butter between thumb and fingers.

Pour in half the water and continue to mix, then add the rest. At this point it should have come together into a robust dough that would hold its shape if cut in half. If too wet, add more flour and mix; if too dry, a touch more water.

Remove from the bowl/machine and knead for a minute or two on a clean surface. Once it has come together into a smooth ball, you can use it directly, but it is preferable to wrap it in cling film and place it in the fridge for 30 minutes to an hour (or up to two days). If the dough becomes too hard when cold, microwave it quickly before use.

When it is time to construct the pies, begin by lining the tins with parchment paper (this is optional but guarantees no stuck and wasted pies). Cut a circle 3–4cm wider than the diameter of each tin. Don't push it into the tin; this is easiest done later.

Roll out the pastry to 3–5mm and, using a parchment circle as a guide, cut out the pastry into rounds.

Place a parchment piece on top of the pie tin, with a circle of pastry on top of that, then use a fist to push it all into the tin. Push it into the corners with your fingers. There should be enough pastry to fold over the lip a bit.

Fill with plentiful chunks of meat and carrot, and top up with gravy, finishing with a slice of cheese.

Cut another circle of pastry large enough to cover the tin and lip. Egg wash the lip and place the pastry on top. Using a downward-facing knife, run it around the outer edge of the lip until you have a neatly shaped pie – you should still have some parchment sticking out, which is very handy for getting the pies out of the tin.

Finally, seal the lid to the pie by forking around the lip (or google crimping techniques for something fancier).

Once all pies are ready, egg wash the top and place on a tray in an oven preheated to 200°C. After 40 minutes, carefully lift one of the pies using the parchment and check that the pastry is cooked. Add another 10–20 minutes, if not.

Remove from the oven and leave to cool on the tray for a few minutes – before they cool completely, remove the pies from the tins by pulling them up with any parchment paper that is sticking out.

Place them back on the tray and either serve or leave in the parchment to cool. Keep any remaining gravy and, if you like, serve this heated in a jug alongside the pie.

Pies will refrigerate well for 3–5 days – to reheat, place in the oven at 200°C for 20 minutes.

Pea and wild garlic risotto

Serves 4

3 shallots, finely chopped,
or 4 spring onions, chopped

60ml olive oil

400g Arborio risotto rice

200ml white wine

800ml vegetable stock

Handful wild garlic, washed
and chopped (you can also
shred a few leaves and reserve
them for the garnish)

400g peas (frozen or fresh)

60g parmesan shavings
(optional)

2 spring onions, finely shredded

The appearance of the ingredients for this recipe are Café Canna's yearly alarm clock that it is time to open up the restaurant. Made from pretty much the first three edible plants to push their way out of the soil every season, it's simple, fresh, vibrant, vegan and ever-popular.

———————

Fry off the shallots in olive oil. They should be really soft, so for at least 10 minutes. Add the rice and stir to coat it in the oil. Let it cook for a minute or two before adding the wine, then turn up the heat a bit.

Once the wine has reduced to almost nothing, add a ladle of the stock. Stir until the liquid has integrated into the rice, then add in some more. Repeat until no stock is left and the rice is al dente – it should be on the cusp of too hard, with a creaminess developing around it.

Add the roughly chopped wild garlic and the peas, then keep on the heat for another minute or two, adding yet more stock if by the end there is still crunch rather than texture to the rice.

Serve with your choice of shaved parmesan, spring onions and some wild garlic scattered on top.

Butter rabbit curry

This dish is our take on one of the finest curries out there – butter chicken. Rabbit is fantastic in curries; you could substitute it in place of chicken in most. There is something about the combination of heat and rich butteriness in this one that is particularly good.

———————

Mix all of the marinade ingredients, then add the rabbit, rubbing the sauce into each portion. Cling film the bowl and place in the fridge overnight ideally.

In a large pot (everything will end up in here), fry the onion in the butter until softened. Add the garlic and ginger and continue to fry for 1 minute, stirring to avoid burning.

Stir in the coriander, garam masala and cumin, then add the tomatoes, chilli powder and some salt.

Simmer for 10–15 minutes, then use a hand blender to blend to a smooth sauce.

In a separate frying pan, on a high heat, add some oil and fry the rabbit pieces – you just want to colour the outside, not cook through. Do this in batches of 2–3, adding to the sauce once done. When all the rabbit is in the sauce, pour in any remaining juices from the frying pan.

Cook for 20–40 minutes, until the rabbit is cooked through and tender, then mix in the cream, sugar and fenugreek leaves, and season with some salt. Continue cooking for 5–10 minutes.

Serve with home-made flatbreads (see p. 216), some rice and pickle, and garnish with, some rice and pickle, chopped coriander.

Serves 4

For the marinade

120ml plain yogurt

2 tbsp garlic (about 6 cloves), finely chopped

1 tbsp ginger, grated

2 tsp garam masala

1 tsp turmeric

1 tsp ground cumin

1 tsp chilli powder

1 tsp salt

800g–1kg rabbit portions (about 1–2 wild rabbits' worth, see p. 170)

For the sauce

30g butter

1 large onion, sliced or chopped

2 tbsp garlic (about 6 cloves), minced

1 tbsp ginger, grated

1 tsp ground coriander

1½ tsp garam masala

1½ tsp ground cumin

400g tin chopped tomatoes

½ tsp red chilli powder

180ml double cream

½ tbsp sugar

½ tsp dried fenugreek leaves

salt

coriander leaves, to garnish

Masala-spiced cauliflower cheese pie

Makes 7 pies
(using 11.5 x 3.5cm tins)

For the pastry

290g soft butter

650g plain flour

½ tsp salt

130ml water

For the filling

2 tbsp olive oil

2 cauliflowers, florets only,
cut down to bite-sized pieces
(they need to fit in the pie,
after all)

1 tsp salt

60g unsalted butter

2 onions, chopped

2 tsp cumin seeds

2 tsp medium curry powder

2 tbsp red chilli flakes

1–2 tsp black mustard seeds

2 tsp Dijon mustard

400–600ml double cream

250g mature cheddar
(we use Isle of Mull), coarsely
grated

1 egg, beaten (to assemble)

This dish started life in response to a couple of things – the gardeners having a glut of cauliflower, and a visit to the island from my mate Tom. He is a vegetarian and loves a pie, things that he often (surprisingly often) complains do not go hand in hand. He's kind of right. Vegetarian pies inexplicably seem to be open, or topped with mash, as if they don't deserve a pastry lid. So I thought I'd see what I could do.

Masala-spiced cauliflower cheese is a huge filling. It's a standalone dish, really. It is exactly the satisfyingly chunky, rich, saucy type of thing that you want to see flooding out of the pastry once it's cracked.

Fully encased in shortcrust pastry (yes, even the top, Tom), this pie started as a special and has been back ever since – it's almost as popular as the beef version.

—————

First, prepare the pastry. In a food mixer (or with your hands), combine the butter, flour and salt. If the butter is not easily malleable, microwave for 20 seconds at a time until it is. If it melts completely, the recipe will work just fine. Mix until very rough breadcrumbs have formed – if using your hands, rub the flour into the butter between thumb and fingers.

Pour in half the water and continue to mix, then add the rest. At this point it should have come together into a robust dough that would hold its shape if cut in half. If too wet, add more flour and mix; if too dry, a touch more water.

Remove from the bowl/machine and knead for a minute or two on a clean surface. Once it has come together into a smooth ball, you can use it directly, but it is preferable to wrap it in cling film and place it in the fridge for 30 minutes to an hour (or up to two days). If the dough becomes too hard when cold, microwave it quickly before use.

SOUP
HOMEMADE BREAD   5

PINT OF LOCAL
LANGOUSTINE
AIOLI, HOMEMADE BREAD
SALAD   19

ON TOAST
HOMEMADE BREAD, POTATO
SALAD, SALA

SANDN
HOMEMADE O
SALAD, SALAD
- MALLAIG
  SALMON,
- ISLAND

PLOUGHMANS
ISLE OF MULL CHEDDAR
PICKLED ONION
CHUTNEY, SALAD, HOMEMADE
BREAD

MALLAIG PEAT-SMOKED
SALMON, SCRAMBLED
ANNA EGGS, TOAST   9

Next, make the filling. Place the florets, olive oil and a good sprinkling of salt in a roasting tray and cover with foil. Place in the oven at 180°C for 30 minutes, or until nice and tender. Set aside.

Fry the onions in the butter until very soft and slightly coloured – 10–20 minutes. Add the cumin, curry powder, chilli flakes and mustard seeds, and fry until they start to pop.

Add the Dijon mustard and the double cream, and combine everything well. Use enough cream to make the filling loose but not excessively thin. Bring the mixture up to almost simmering, then add the cheese and season, if necessary.

Let this cool completely before pie assembly.

Assembling the pie

Follow exactly the same assembly instructions as for the beef pie (pp. 178–79). Just make sure each of these pies gets a good quantity of both cauliflower and sauce.

Once all pies are ready, egg wash the top and place on a tray in an oven preheated to 200°C for 40 minutes. Carefully lift one using the parchment to check that the pastry is cooked – add another 10–20 minutes, if not.

Once cooked, remove from the oven and leave to cool on the tray for a few minutes – but before they cool completely, remove from the tin by pulling up by any parchment that is sticking out. Place back on the tray and either serve or leave in the parchment to cool. Serve with a creamy mash and seasonal greens.

Pies will refrigerate well for 3–5 days. To reheat, place in the oven at 200°C for 20 minutes.

Curry mutton

Serves 4–5

1 tbsp black peppercorns

10 cardamom pods

1 tbsp fenugreek seeds

1 cinnamon stick

1 bunch (150g) coriander

1 tbsp ground coriander

1 tbsp ground ginger

1 tbsp ground turmeric

3 garlic cloves, finely chopped

400g tin tomatoes

1 tbsp chilli flakes (or to taste)

a couple of sprigs or 2 tsp dried thyme

3 tbsp HP sauce

sunflower oil or butter, for frying

2kg shoulder mutton, significant sinew/fat removed and diced into big egg-sized chunks (any other cut of mutton will do fine, by the way)

2 onions, finely chopped

1 tsp salt

Cooked in the Caribbean way, this traditional West Indian curry, rich in spice and tang, is a great way to showcase mutton, bursting with flavour and so tender it is falling to bits. You could very easily do this with lamb – or, if you can get it, goat – but mutton is best. You can also buy the spice mix, ready prepared (it's called Jamaican curry blend).

As the recipe calls for the meat to be marinaded overnight, you probably want to start this the day before you're intending to make it.

In a dry pan, fry the peppercorns, cardamom, fenugreek and cinnamon until aromatic, then grind either in a coffee grinder (I use this), or with a pestle and mortar.

Chop the coriander stalks and set the leaves aside. Combine the chopped stalks, the ground spices and all of the other ingredients, except the onion, in a large bowl and mix well. Get your hands in to massage the marinade into the meat. Leave overnight.

Remove the meat from the marinade (but keep the marinade) and, in a very hot pan, with a touch of oil, and working in batches, brown all over and set aside.

In a pot big enough to hold everything, fry the onions in some oil for 10–15 minutes until very soft and slightly coloured, then add the meat and marinade. Add enough water to cover the meat and bring to a gentle simmer.

On probably the lowest heat, cover and keep it slowly bubbling away until the meat easily falls apart (3–4 hours), stirring every so often. For a thick sauce, remove the lid towards the end and let it reduce down.

Add a teaspoon or so of salt, and serve with rice and some pickle. Scatter the reserved coriander leaves on top.

Canna cassoulet

For the confit rabbit

1 rabbit, jointed (see p. 170 for instructions)

500ml (or enough to cover the rabbit) sunflower oil

For the beans

1kg haricot or cannellini beans, soaked in cold water overnight (or bring to the boil, soak for 40 minutes, drain and rinse)

1 onion, peeled and spiked with 4 cloves each

4 garlic cloves, peeled

2 tsp thyme

2 bay leaves

Any excess fat from the mutton (don't bother chopping it)

For the cassoulet

1 large onion, chopped

3 garlic cloves, chopped

400g tin tomatoes

1 tbsp tomato puree

1kg mutton, large chunks

500g (or more – I probably would) venison sausages

500ml chicken stock

The definitive recipe for the French peasant classic, cassoulet, is hotly debated, but it tends to be a variation on a rich, meaty, beany theme. This is our version, using island ingredients where possible. In place of confit duck, we use rabbit; instead of pork belly, mutton; and instead of the usual Toulouse sausages, we use venison ones.

It is an indulgent dish that almost certainly needs a day or two (both to cook and eat, perhaps), but is quick and easy to serve, needing no side other than a simple green salad and perhaps a slice of bread to mop up the thick, flavourful sauce at the end.

There are many options for substitution here – you could easily swap back to the more traditional meats if preferred/easier. The directions are the same. I'd recommend making a big batch of this – it will freeze well.

To make the confit rabbit, in a single layer pack the meat and joints from the rabbit into an ovenproof dish. Just cover with sunflower oil and place in the oven at 130°C. After 3–4 hours, remove the rabbit from the oil – keep the legs whole and break the rest of the meat off the bone into chunks.

Meanwhile, drain the beans and add to a large pan. Cover with water to 3cm above the bean level. Add the onion, garlic, herbs and mutton fat. Bring to the boil, then cover and simmer for about 2 hours until just tender but not falling apart (you want it to be a bit thick and saucy). Remove the onion, cloves, garlic and fat.

For the cassoulet, in a pan large enough to fit everything, soften the onion and garlic. Add the tin of tomatoes and the tomato puree and simmer gently for 20 minutes to a rich and thick sauce.

Next, working in batches, brown the mutton and sausages in a very hot frying pan, adding them to the tomato sauce when browned.

Add the beans, plus some of their juice (if there is a lot, don't add it all), and enough chicken stock to cover, then check the seasoning (add some if necessary but it may be quite salty already). Bring to a simmer and reduce to the lowest heat. Cook for 2–4 hours, until the mutton is very tender and will fall to bits easily.

Add the confit rabbit and heat through.

Serve with simple salad and some good home-made bread.

Rabbit stew

A classic Café Canna dish, rabbit stew was once as synonymous with the restaurant as seafood is now. It still makes an honorary appearance on occasion.

I would heartily encourage the use of more rabbit in cooking. A lean, healthy, slightly gamey meat, it can be adapted to many chicken-based recipes – and in my opinion, it makes them just a little more interesting. This dish is based on wild rabbit, which does need more time in the pot to tenderise than farmed. If that's what you have bought, though, there are easy adjustments below.

For step-by-step instructions on how to joint a rabbit, see page 170.

Before you brown the rabbit pieces, first dust the meat in 2–3 tablespoons of flour. Next, in batches, fry in a very hot pan with a little oil until the outside is coloured. Once each piece is done, place it in a bowl, and when all of it is finished, deglaze the pan with a glug of red wine – it will bubble and helps to extract all of the delicious flavour left behind. Pour/scrape this into the reserved bowl of rabbit pieces.

In a pot large enough to take all the ingredients, on a medium heat, fry the onion in the butter until soft (10 minutes). Add the celery and carrot and continue for another 5 minutes. Add 2 tablespoons of flour and the Dijon mustard, and mix it into a slight paste, then continue to cook for 5 minutes.

Add the browned rabbit, the stock, thyme and enough red wine to cover the rabbit by 3–4cm.

Bring to a simmer and then reduce to a very low simmer (probably minimum heat). Cover and cook for 2–3 hours (1–2 hours, if you are using farmed rabbit), stirring and checking its tenderness occasionally.

Once the meat is almost falling off the bone, add the salt to taste and serve with a creamy mash (p. 225) and greens (p. 223).

Serves 4–6

2 rabbits, jointed

4–5 tbsp plain flour

20g butter

2 onions, chopped

4 celery sticks, sliced chunkily on the diagonal

4 large carrots, sliced chunkily on the diagonal

1 tbsp Dijon mustard

1 litre chicken stock

1 tbsp thyme

1 litre red wine (or enough to cover)

1–2 tsp salt

Beef (and dulse skirlie) olives

Serves 4

For the olives

50g butter

1 large onion, finely chopped

½ beef stock cube

150g of pinhead oatmeal, or medium oatmeal

salt and freshly ground black pepper

4 tbsp dulse flakes, or a handful of chopped fresh (or rehydrated) dulse

4 rump or 'minute' steaks, bashed to ½cm thickness

4 tsp Dijon mustard

For the sauce

a good glug of olive oil

1 onion, chopped

2 large carrots, chopped

300ml beef stock

100ml red wine

1 tbsp plain flour

salt and freshly ground black pepper

The confusingly named beef olives (I have no idea why they're called 'olives') have been a favourite of mine since childhood; they are thin slices of beef that are rolled up with a filling inside, then slow cooked in a rich sauce or gravy until tender and steeped in flavour. The combination of the tender juicy steak and the filling that has by then soaked up a good whack of the sauce is incredible, homely and delicious.

There are usually two varieties, neither of which contains olives: one is filled with sausage meat, the other is filled with a traditional Scottish oatmeal stuffing known as skirlie. I am personally only interested in the latter.

Our version takes skirlie and adds dulse, which adds a slightly bacon-like twist to the original, retaining the absorption of the skirlie whilst bringing in some of the meatiness of the sausage variety.

———

First, make the dulse skirlie. Melt the butter in a pan and soften the onion. Add the half stock cube, then the oatmeal, and stir to thoroughly coat with the onions. Season well and reduce heat to a minimum. Cook for 20–25 minutes until the oatmeal has softened. Add the dulse and let it cool.

Lay out the flattened, bashed thin steaks, smear the upper side with mustard, then place a sausage of the skirlie at one end a few centimetres from the edge. Roll it up in the beef, tucking the sides in as you go, so that the skirlie is completely sealed in. Use some string to tie it up.

For the sauce, place the onion and carrots in a large, high-sided oven tray with a glug or two of oil and bake at 180°C for 40 minutes, stirring once or twice. Add the stock, wine and the prepared olives, and cover with foil. Cook at 170°C for 2–3 hours until tender.

Set the olives aside and strain the liquid into a pan, then reduce by half. For a thicker sauce, whisk in the flour.

Serve with some creamy mash and perhaps a nice simple side, with a generous dousing of the reduced sauce.

Mutton shanks

The shank of mutton can be huge. These make for a sizable main course. It's a classic dish, made better with the depth of flavour that comes with mutton rather than lamb, and it's one of our (and our customers') favourites. It's not a cut that you get many of, so it's a real treat to be able to make and eat this.

In a pot large enough to hold the shanks neatly, heat some sunflower oil and add the onion. Fry on a medium heat for 10 minutes until soft, then add the garlic, carrots and celery. Continue cooking for another 5 minutes.

Add the wine (save a glug for deglazing the pan), tomatoes, tomato paste, stock, thyme and bay leaves, and bring to a simmer.

In a separate pan, on a high heat, add a good few glugs of sunflower oil. Sear the shanks one or two at a time all over, and once coloured add to the pot with everything else.

Once all the shanks are in, deglaze the frying pan by sloshing a little red wine about, with the pan still hot. Add all the juices collected to the big pot. Gently simmer, ensuring the shanks are completely covered, for 2–2½ hours, until the meat is falling off the bone (but they're still together).

Remove the shanks, then increase the heat and reduce the sauce that's left by about a quarter.

Serve the warmed shanks with some creamy mash, a good dousing of the sauce and some simple veg – we like sautéed red cabbage or cumin and honey roast carrots (p. 223).

Serves 4

sunflower oil, for frying

1 onion, finely chopped

4 garlic cloves, finely chopped

2 large carrots, peeled and finely chopped

2 celery sticks, finely chopped

1 bottle red wine

2 x 400g tins tomatoes

2 tbsp tomato paste

500ml chicken stock

1 tbsp dried thyme

2 bay leaves

4 mutton shanks (or lamb, if you can't get mutton)

Beetroot and mushroom bourguignon

Serves 4

olive oil, for frying

2 medium white onions, chopped

6 garlic cloves, finely chopped

1kg beetroot, peeled and cut into thick wedges

4 large carrots, peeled and cut into thick batons

4 bay leaves

2 tbsp thyme

300ml red wine

1 litre vegetable stock

2 tbsp tomato puree

100g pearl barley

4 red onions, peeled and quartered

500g chestnut mushrooms

This is a vegan dish that will warm any heart and satisfy the most ardent carnivore. It is hugely rich and meaty-seeming. Beetroot is a vegetable that does incredibly well over in our veg patch, and it's great to make a star out of a really underutilised crop.

Fry the white onions in olive oil until softened and then add the garlic and continue to fry for a further minute. Add everything else, except the red onions and the mushrooms, and bring to a simmer. Leave for 40–50 minutes until the beetroot is tender.

Meanwhile fry the red onions and the mushrooms until they have coloured on the outside, then add them to the pot.

Serve with a good creamy mash (p. 225).

Rabbit and chutney sausage roll

This is a great way to try out rabbit for the first time, and it's a nice option for a snack, or lunch, or to pack in a picnic.

Try and make these chunky – you can make the diddly cocktail size if you like, but to get the real meaty feel it works much better with a high meat-to-pastry ratio!

For step-by-step instructions on jointing a rabbit, see page 170.

———————

First, prepare the rabbit meat. If you can buy it deboned, there is no need for this step – simply chop very finely. Cooking the rabbit first makes it much easier to remove the meat from the bones. Roast at 180°C for 40 minutes, then once cool enough to handle remove the meat and chop finely.

Sweat the red onion in a frying pan with a glug of sunflower oil until soft, then add the garlic for a further minute. Combine the onion, garlic, sausage meat, rabbit, thyme, wholegrain mustard and a teaspoon of salt, and mix well.

Lay out the puff pastry – if you are using the bought, rolled type, roll the whole thing out. You'll construct it in long rolls and cut to size later, so the width should be 10–15cm.

Spoon a generous line of chutney down the centre of the pastry, then form a sausage out of the meat mixture on top of that. Make sure it's not so fat that the pastry won't overlap when the sides are folded up. Fold one whole side of pastry up, then test that the other folds up, with at least 1cm overlap. If it doesn't, either remove some meat or cut away excess pastry.

Place the other flap back down and brush the overlapping edge with egg, then fold it back again. Place a sheet of parchment on a baking tray.

Cut the now formed but uncooked sausage roll into desired lengths and place, overlapping side down, on the tray. Brush with egg. Cook in a preheated oven at 180°C for 40 minutes, or until golden and piping hot right through.

Makes 10–12 large sausage rolls

1 rabbit, jointed

sunflower oil, for frying

1 red onion, finely chopped

3 garlic cloves, finely chopped

500g sausage meat

1 tbsp dried thyme

1 tbsp wholegrain mustard

1 tsp salt

600g puff pastry sheets

200ml chutney (we often go for apple and plum)

1 egg, beaten

Wild garlic and brie pasty

Makes 6–8 pasties

650g shortcrust pastry

150g white potatoes, cut into
small dice

50g carrots, cut into small dice

150g brie, cut into small chunks

70g wild garlic, cleaned and
roughly chopped

1 tbsp flour

4 tbsp milk

salt and freshly ground black
pepper

1 egg, beaten

This is a lovely way to enjoy the perilously short season but abundant glut of wild garlic. We make these with a fantastic brie from the Connage Highland Dairy in Inverness-shire. Almost any other brie or cheese would do, however – our home-made crowdie would be fantastic.

We use shortcrust pastry for simplicity, but if you're buying it, try the recipe with puff pastry instead, if you like.

To make the pastry, follow the instructions on page 184. If using shop-bought pastry, follow the instructions on the label.

In a bowl, combine the potatoes, carrots, brie, wild garlic, flour and milk and season well.

Roll out the pastry on a floured surface and cut into circles, perhaps 15–20cm across. Scoop out a good handful of the filling and place it in the centre of each circle of pastry.

Brush the pastry's perimeter with egg and fold one side over to form a semicircle. A bit of trial and error will be required to get the right amount of filling for your chosen pasty size, however there should be 1–2cm of lip around the edge – compress this together.

Seal by pushing a fork end down along the lip or by crimping. To do this well, it might help to watch a video online, but with the lip side facing right, place your rightmost thumb at the furthest edge, then fold a small portion of the lip back on that thumb with your left fingers. Move down a centimetre and repeat, so that you're pushing with your thumb and folding with your left hand.

Once all the pasties are sealed and ready, brush with egg and place on a baking tray. Cook in a preheated oven at 180°C for 40 minutes, or until golden.

Isle of Mull cheddar macaroni pies

This is our version of one of the finest things to come out of the North-east: the carbohydrate bomb that is the macaroni pie. That's right, I often have to explain to visiting friends, it is a pie filled with macaroni cheese. What's odd about that? One of the principal reasons to go out on the boat is the excuse to eat one of these, but, reduced in size, they also make a really popular buffet option. The recipe is based on making the smaller-sized pies, but these can easily be upscaled.

Cook the pasta, as per the instructions on the packet, then drain and set aside.

Melt the butter in a saucepan and add the garlic. Let it sizzle for a minute. Still on the heat, add the flour and mix into a roux. Add the milk a good slosh at a time, ensuring it is absorbed before adding more. Once it's fully combined, reduce the heat to low and continue cooking until it has thickened to a white sauce. Add the mustard and the cheddar (keep aside a little for topping the pies), some salt and combine again. Add most of the pasta and, if there's still plenty of sauce, add the rest.

Now, to assemble the pies. Grease the muffin moulds with butter, cut a circle of pastry with a pastry cutter (10–11cm in diameter, if you have one, or use any sort of circular object to guide you) and place the pastry in each of the moulds.

Add the macaroni cheese so that it fills and mounds up beyond the height of the mould. Sprinkle some spare cheddar on top and season with a grind of pepper. Place in a preheated oven at 180°C for 30 minutes, or until the cheese is lightly coloured and the pastry is fully cooked.

Makes 18–24 mini pies

250g macaroni pasta

40g butter

2 garlic cloves, finely chopped

2 tbsp plain flour

350ml whole milk

2 tsp Dijon mustard

250g cheddar, grated

600g puff pastry sheets

½ tsp salt and a good few grinds of black pepper

Nettle and spinach spanakopita

Serves 6

200g nettles, stalks removed

500g spinach

1 leek, finely sliced

small bunch parsley, chopped

small bunch mint (leaves only), chopped

small bunch dill, chopped

sprinkle nutmeg

100ml or so of olive oil

1kg pack filo pastry (for vegan, make sure it is oil-based rather than butter-based)

200g feta (optional)

salt and freshly ground black pepper

I used to live beside a Greek bakery and could never resist getting a slice of this. Spanakopita is a pie made with filo pastry, plenty of olive oil and strongly herbed vegetables. Once I'd arrived on Canna, and with spinach, parsley, dill and mint growing aplenty just over the wall from us, it was one mainland snack I couldn't wait to recreate.

Our version contains nettles, which add a punchiness and pepperiness that spinach alone lacks, but can be omitted if preferred.

Many brands of shop-bought filo are vegan-friendly. Omit the feta and this makes a fantastic vegan dish. (The Greek bakery sold two versions of spanakopita, with and without feta, and I loved them equally.)

In a pan of boiling water, blanch the nettles for a minute, then drain in a colander. Add the spinach into the same colander and toss in some salt. Leave for 30 minutes. Squeeze to extract as much liquid as possible and transfer to a bowl.

Mix in the leek, herbs, nutmeg, seasoning and a glug of olive oil.

Brush a high-sided oven tray (somewhere around 25 x 35cm) with oil. Layer about 8 sheets (or half the pack, if you have less) of filo into the tray, brushing each with olive oil before adding the next. If larger than the vessel (preferable), have the pastry go up the sides.

Add the mixture to fill the pie, then (if using) crumble the feta on top. Fold any overlaps on top.

Layer another 8 sheets (or the other half of the pack, if less) of filo on top, again with a generous brushing of oil between each, tucking down the sides, if larger than the vessel.

Brush the top with oil and sprinkle with a bit of water.

Bake at 175°C for 50 minutes to an hour. Cut into squares and serve whilst still warm (the best), or serve later either cold or reheated (both still delicious).

Potato and wild mint salad

Serves 6–10

1kg new potatoes

1 tbsp red wine vinegar

1 tbsp wholegrain mustard

½ red onion, or 3 spring onions, very finely sliced

3 tbsp capers

25g parsley, chopped

50g wild mint leaves, chopped

3–4 tbsp mayonnaise

salt and freshly ground black pepper

We serve this with just about every daytime dish – we (the staff) eat troughs of it and still love it. You can go fancier with the ingredients and there are many options for substitutions or additions, but I would say the mint is as important as the tatties and the mayo – don't skip that.

———

Boil the potatoes until just tender – they should be hard, but not crunchy. Cool by running cold water into the pan.

Cut the potatoes in half (or thirds, if large) and place in a bowl big enough to take everything. Add the remaining ingredients, except the mayonnaise, and mix.

Now add the mayo, starting with 3 tbsp to see if it's to your liking. Add more, if not. Season well with salt and pepper.

Pea and wild mint soup

A fresh, wholesome soup that perfectly encapsulates spring, when these two ingredients are amongst the first to arrive. Once you have the ingredients – and it works equally well with frozen peas – it is amongst the quickest and easiest to put together.

In a large pot, soften the onion in the olive oil for 10 minutes. Add the garlic and cook for a further minute. Add in the peas, mint and the stock. Simmer for 15 minutes or until the peas have softened, then whizz with a hand blender. Serve with good bread.

Serves 4

a glug of olive oil

2 onions, roughly chopped

1 garlic clove, roughly chopped

1kg peas

125g wild mint leaves, roughly chopped

1.5 litres vegetable stock

ACCOMPANIMENTS

Trusty, crusty, everyday white loaf

Anna's mum's oatcakes

Flatbreads

Rhubarb, cannellini bean and potato bake

Simple salad with a vinaigrette

Honey and cummin roast carrots

Creamy (sometimes wholegrain mustard) mash

Trusty, crusty, everyday white loaf

Every morning starts with baking bread. It's a very important part of the operation and one that we rely on turning out well. This particular loaf has been honed over the years to be extremely quick and reliable to make, with a fluffy, chewy-crusted outcome.

When you start to make bread, there can be some worry at a few stages: Has it been kneaded enough? Was the rise sufficient? – that kind of thing. Perhaps it's worth knowing now that it is almost impossible to stuff this up completely. Time spent kneading will increase the quality of the loaf by a gradient that starts at pretty great, for instance. My advice is: make the loaf and tailor the time spent on it to you. When practised, it shouldn't take more than 20 minutes of your time in total.

Ideally you'll have a bread tin and a food mixer with paddle attachment, but neither are necessary.

———

Put all the dry ingredients in the mixer, or into a large bowl, and combine. Add the water.

If using a mixer, set to a low speed and continue even once the dough has centred (which means as long as some of it is touching the bottom of the bowl) for a good 10 minutes until the dough is quite smooth.

If mixing by hand, use the tips of your fingers to combine, then start to knead in the bowl until fully combined, moving the dough around to incorporate any straggling flour. The bowl should be completely clean by the time you're done.

Once ready, turn out onto a clean surface and knead (stretch it away from you with one palm, then fold and repeat) until the dough springs back when prodded and there are no dry patches when stretching out. The more you do this, the better (up to about 20 minutes), but even without kneading at all you'll still get a nice loaf.

600g bread flour (plain flour works, if that is what you have)

8.5g instant yeast

1 tsp sugar

1 tsp salt

400ml warm (not boiling) water

Place the dough back in the bowl it came from and cover loosely with cling film or a tea towel.

Place in a warm area in the kitchen, or beside the fire or a heater, to rise to at least double the size. If it over-rises (and starts to fall) this is OK at this stage.

Grease the bread tin, if using, by rubbing with olive oil.

Turn the dough out onto a surface and push it down flat to remove the air. Mould it into a fat sausage a bit smaller than the size of your tin. Place it into the bread tin – or, if you don't have one, onto a baking sheet.

Rise the dough again, for approximately 20–30 minutes, to the top of the tin. Place in an oven preheated to 220°C for 15 minutes, then reduce to 190°C and bake for a further 30 minutes.

As soon as you can handle it when it comes out of the oven, remove from the tin and turn over to allow the bottom to steam/dry.

If you don't use all of the bread that day, you can perhaps make it into breadcrumbs for the croquettes (p. 47), or they freeze quite well.

Anna's mum's oatcakes

Anna (from Canna)'s mum, Irene, makes fantastic oatcakes. They are healthy, straightforward and delicious. We use these on our cheese boards, but they also make extremely good vessels for our home-made crowdie (p. 53).

Mix the dry ingredients and make a well in the middle. Pour in the olive oil and combine, then add the boiling water and mix into a slightly sticky ball. If it's too sticky to handle, add more oats.

To roll it out, flour a work surface - or, probably better, sprinkle with oatmeal. Roll to any thickness, from 1cm to really quite chunky (my preference), then cut into squares with either a knife or a circular cutter.

Place on a baking tray that has been lightly sprinkled with oatmeal (or flour) and bake for 20 minutes at 180 C, then turn them over and bake for another 20 minutes. If they start to break when turning, place back in for another 10 minutes.

Makes a baking tray or so of oatcakes

140g medium oatmeal

140g porridge oats

1 tsp salt

75ml olive oil

100–120ml (approx.) boiling water

Flatbreads

450 self-raising flour

1 tsp baking powder

300g yoghurt

50ml water

Some dishes – spiced dishes, most obviously – are better accompanied by flatbreads. These are super quick and easy. If you have ever been disappointed by a cold or soggy naan, or need bread but do not have time for the rising/proving routine, making these is an almost instant solution.

———————

Mix the dry ingredients together, then add the yogurt and water.

Use your hands to combine and then knead the dough, moving to a floured surface once it has come together.

Divide into 6 or 8 balls, then roll them out to 1cm thick.

Heat a dry frying pan and place the rolled out dough into it on a medium to high heat. Fry on one side for a few minutes until the bread can be easily picked up with tongs. Flip every few minutes, looking for a small amount of charring but not excessive burning on each side.

Pile onto a plate and either use immediately or heat in the oven later.

Rhubarb, cannellini bean and potato bake

The tart sharpness of rhubarb in this recipe goes extremely well with any mackerel or other oily fish dish (we serve it with the kelp-wrapped mackerel on page 74). It is also a good side for vegan dishes – a vegetable stew or roast celeriac, for example. We usually make this in a high-sided roasting tin (approximately 32 x 22cm).

———

Place all the ingredients, except the rhubarb and the beans, into the roasting tin and combine. Bake in the oven at 220°C for 30 minutes. Once it's ready, stir and add in the rhubarb and the beans. Bake for a further 15 minutes.

Serves 8–10

750g potatoes, washed but not peeled, sliced into 1cm rounds

1 tbsp dried rosemary

4 bay leaves

2 tbsp fennel seeds

4 tbsp white wine vinegar

3 tbsp honey

a good glug of olive oil

250g rhubarb, cut into thick diagonal slices

400g tin cannellini beans

Simple salad with a vinaigrette

Serves 4

For bramble vinegar

300g brambles (or other berries)

300ml white wine or cider vinegar

70g sugar

For a vinaigrette

80ml olive oil

2 tbsp Dijon mustard

1 tsp honey

30ml red wine vinegar (or the home-made bramble variety above)

salt and freshly ground black pepper

For the veg

1 carrot, cut into shavings using a potato peeler

1 courgette, cut into shavings using a potato peeler

3–4 handfuls of leaf – lambs lettuce, little gem, whatever is in season

6 cherry tomatoes, halved

6 radishes, sliced

a few tiny sprigs of a herb – dill, perhaps

Many of the dishes in this book call for simple accompaniments. Big seafood dishes require nothing more than mayo, tasty bread and perhaps a few ideas from here.

Fruit vinegar is one of my favourite ways to contribute something home-made to the sprucing up of a standard (but difficult to beat) vinaigrette. It's also a fantastic way to use up and preserve a glut of berries. Raspberries work really well, as do brambles, which are prolific on the island.

Obviously, everybody knows how to make a salad, and all the ingredients are debatable and interchangeable.

———————

To make the bramble (or other fruit) vinegar (approximately 200–300ml), mash the brambles a bit and add to a jar or bottle with the vinegar. Leave for 3–10 days (the longer, the better), giving it a shake every now and then. Drain the liquid into a pan through a muslin or sieve, add the sugar and simmer for 10 minutes. Place directly into sterilised jars or bottles and store in a dark place – use after a few weeks and within six months.

Alternatively, to make a simple vinaigrette, add the ingredients to a jar or bowl, with a good seasoning of salt and freshly ground black pepper, and shake or stir well.

Bring everything together by combining the veg and herbs, and pouring the fruit vinegar or vinaigrette over the salad at the last moment possible before serving.

Honey and cumin roast carrots

This is a fantastic side to any meat dish but goes especially well with the pies. (It looks great, too.) You really want decent-sized carrots for this. You can leave them big – whole, even, depending on your preference.

———

Place everything in a roasting tin. Combine the honey, oil, cummin and salt. Then rub the carrots with the oil, honey and cumin mix, then cover tightly with tin foil. Roast at 210°C for 40–50 minutes.

Serves 4

8 large carrots, peeled, stalk end removed and halved lengthways (or left whole)

a good squeeze of runny honey

a good glug of olive oil

1 tsp cumin

½ tsp salt

Creamy (sometimes wholegrain mustard) mash

Serves 4

1kg potatoes, peeled and chunked (any floury variety – Maris Piper, King Edward, etc.)

250ml whole milk

125g butter

1–2 tsp wholegrain mustard (optional)

salt and freshly ground black pepper

To make a good mashed potato takes love and effort. It is not an easy win, nor will it ever be part of a diet plan, but the result is just gorgeous. It should be silky smooth, creamy, almost sauce-like, but with structure enough to stay put in its dollop. It is the correct accompaniment to a good pie. A potato ricer is an almost essential addition to any mash-making kitchen – if you love your mash and don't have one, consider buying one.

———————

Boil the potatoes in salty water until soft but not breaking apart. At the same time, heat the milk and butter in another pan to almost a simmer.

It is important that the potatoes are kept as hot as possible during the next step, so have everything ready and ensure the milk/butter is up to temperature.

Drain the cooked potatoes into a colander, then immediately rice them back into the pan they came from. Add about half the hot milk and stir. Add the rest gradually, ensuring that the potatoes do not become too sloppy. It will seem almost certain that there is too much for the potatoes to soak up, but keep stirring and adding and, depending a little on the potatoes used, it should all get absorbed.

Taste and season. If using, mix in the wholegrain mustard at this stage and serve.

SWEET THINGS

Talisker whisky and honey ice cream

Shortbread

Mrs Carnie's date and walnut cake

Rum (from Rum) baba

Wild gorse crème brûlée

Wild thyme and mint ice cream

Apple tarte tatin

Cranachan baked alaska

Sea buckthorn sorbet

Talisker whisky and honey ice cream

The self-created challenge in this recipe was to find out how much whisky we could get in yet still make the ice cream freeze. When serving alcohol in the bar was banned during lockdown, we briefly, considered whether this dish might become some sort of loophole.

Talisker is a perfect whisky for this ice cream. It happens to be our most locally distilled malt – made just over the water in Carbost on Skye. It is smoky, but not too much so – just enough to really complement the honey and cream.

As with most ice creams, you can get away with not using an ice cream machine; it just adds the requirement to stir it regularly whilst freezing.

Whisk the cream and the whiskies together until the mixture is well whipped and holding its form.

In a pan, bring the honey to boiling point and remove from the heat.

Whisking very vigorously as you go, very slowly pour the yolks into the newly off-the-heat honey (you really need to put some effort in or you will end up with scrambled eggs in honey). When fully combined, it should be smooth and creamy.

Gently fold the yolk/honey mixture into the whisky cream.

Place the mixture into an ice-cream machine and churn until frozen, or place in an ice-cream tub in the freezer and stir every 30 minutes or so until set.

Serve with shortbread – ideally home-made (see p. 230) – and a drizzle of honey.

Makes 1–2 litres

1 litre double cream

130ml Talisker single malt

60ml non-peaty whisky (we use Glenlivet)

190ml runny honey

13 egg yolks, whisked

Shortbread

Makes approx. 10 shortbread
biscuits

60g caster sugar
(plus more to finish)

120g unsalted butter,
at room temperature

1 pinch salt

130g plain flour

30g rice flour

Shortbread is surprisingly quick and easy to put together, lasts a long time and is something that is sure to impress anyone popping in for tea, or as part of a dessert. We put rice flour in ours for that extra crumbly – almost sandy – texture. We serve it with our honey and whisky ice cream (see p. 229).

Preheat the oven to 170°C.

Beat the sugar and butter together until pale and creamy.

Mix in the salt, flour and rice flour.

Place parchment paper on a baking tray and either roll out the dough (to about 1cm), cut into squares and add to the tray – or do all of this directly on the tray to save a bit of time. Bake for 20 minutes.

Sprinkle with more sugar, then leave to cool.

Mrs Carnie's date and walnut cake

We bake cakes daily at the restaurant and we all know this recipe off by heart, so quickly does it need replenishing. Sticky, sweet and moist, but with the crunch of walnuts – it's our most popular cake for good reason.

Fiona (Mrs Carnie) is also a talented potter. If you're enjoying this cake at Café Canna, you'll almost certainly have one of her beautiful handmade cups in front of you, too.

Place the dates and bicarbonate of soda in a bowl, mix in 240ml of boiling water and let it sit whilst completing the next step.

Cream the butter and sugar, then add the egg, chopped walnuts, self-raising flour, vanilla essence and the date mixture and combine well.

Grease a baking tin or line it with parchment paper, then bake at 180°C for 35 minutes – or until a knife comes out clean.

Place the topping ingredients in a pan and stir on the heat until they are melted and combined, then pour over the cake whilst it's still hot – it will run over the cake and should melt into it a bit.

200g chopped dates

1 tsp bicarbonate of soda

240ml boiling water

100g butter

225g sugar

1 egg

80g chopped walnuts

300g self-raising flour

½ tsp vanilla essence

For the topping

5 tbsp brown sugar

2 tbsp butter

2 tbsp milk

Rum (from Rum) baba

Serves 4

For the rum-soaked raisins

6 tbsp golden raisins

200ml dark rum (Rum's Askival, or a dark Caribbean rum)

For the soaking liquor

500g brown sugar

2 tsp vanilla extract

500ml water

250ml dark rum (if you happen to have some of Rum's Askival, use it half and half with another Caribbean rum, like Kraken)

For the babas

5g dried yeast

3 tsp brown sugar

200g plain flour

1 tsp salt

2 eggs, beaten

75g butter (softened until almost liquid)

When our nearest neighbour, the Isle of Rum, started making rum, we immediately wanted to incorporate it in our menu – and given the rum retention qualities of a baba, it seemed a natural fit. Rum baba hardly needs an introduction: a dense sponge soaked to bursting point in a rum liquor, it is rightly a classic. In this case, served with raisins (also soaked to the skin in rum). You'll need a standard muffin tray for these.

Soak the raisins in the rum overnight.

To make the liquor, dissolve the sugar and vanilla into the water in a pan on a medium heat. Once completely integrated, take it off the heat and let cool. Once cooled, add the rum and set aside.

To make the babas, first activate the yeast by placing it in 75ml warm water, with a teaspoon of the sugar (it should start to bubble – there's something wrong with the yeast, if not).

Combine the flour, the remaining sugar and the salt, then add in the yeast mixture. Stir as you go, add the eggs slowly, then the butter, and combine well.

Fill the muffin moulds to two-thirds or three-quarters full and leave to rise.

Heat the oven to 160°C. Once risen, place the babas in the oven for approximately 20 minutes until a skewer comes out clean.

Turn the babas over in the muffin moulds and let cool.

Before serving, soak the babas in the liquor for 30 minutes to an hour, heating as you go, if you like (I prefer them cold). Plate up the now soaked baba and pour some more liquor over the top, followed by a sprinkling of rum-soaked raisins. Add a dollop of cream or a scoop of ice cream.

Wild gorse crème brûlée

Like many locations in Scotland, we are lucky enough to have plentiful wild gorse. When it is in full season, you can smell it from miles away – it has an absolutely gorgeous aroma and one that makes the island feel properly tropical (did I mention there were white sandy beaches and turquoise waters here too?).

Of all the wild flowers, it is this one that we were most keen on capturing in a dish. It's not an easy thing to collect or store, but by creating a syrup, and using prickle-avoidance techniques, it is possible to do both without too much hassle (or broken skin). The gorse syrup needs to infuse for 12–24 hours so should be made in advance.

To make a good crème brûlée, you really need a blow torch. It is possible to get a good result using the grill, but if you're going to make many I'd highly recommend trying to source one. Also required are some (decent-sized) ramekins. You can use a standard bowl if stuck, it just means you'll have a lot of surface area – so lots of scorched crunchy sugar (not necessarily a bad thing!).

When you are ready to make the crème brûlée, preheat the oven to 150°C. Boil a full kettle. Place the sugar, cream and gorse syrup in a pan and heat until the sugar dissolves.

Whisk the yolks in a large bowl, then continue to whisk in the cream/sugar/syrup mixture to the yolks. Pass through a sieve into a jug. Pour the mixture into ramekins and place them into a deep roasting tin filled with the boiling water (make sure it goes halfway to two-thirds of the way up the ramekins).

Place into the heated oven for 30–40 minutes. Check after 30 minutes – they should be wobbly but not liquid. Remove from the oven and leave in the tin for 10 minutes, then remove from the water and cool completely.

To serve, scatter sugar on top and heat with a blow torch to form a crunchy sugar top.

Serves approx. 4–6

35g caster sugar

400ml double cream

120ml gorse syrup
(see p. 159)

6 egg yolks

approx. 5 tbsp sugar, to serve

Wild thyme and mint ice cream

Serves 4-6

500ml double cream

275ml milk

a small bunch of wild mint, cleaned and leaves only

a small bunch of wild thyme, cleaned with stalks

9 egg yolks

200g caster sugar

This ice cream is made out of two of our favourite herbs, both found quite handily in abundance just along the track from the restaurant. This is a creamy yet fresh ice cream that is a lovely refreshing end to a meal. It also goes beautifully with very rich desserts (sticky toffee pudding or chocolate torte, say).

———————

Add the cream, milk, mint and thyme to a pot and bring almost to a simmer, then remove from the heat and leave to infuse for 1–2 hours.

Whisk the egg yolks and sugar in a separate bowl (you'll add the milk to this in a moment).

Sieve the mint and thyme out of the milk, then reheat to simmer point.

Whisking vigorously, slowly integrate the warm milk into the yolks.

On a low heat, stir until a thick custard has formed, then remove from the heat and let it cool.

If you have an ice-cream maker, churn it until it's frozen, otherwise decant into a tub and place in a freezer, stirring every 30 minutes until set.

Serve garnished with a sprig of mint and a few leaves of thyme.

Apple tarte tatin

We're very lucky to have an orchard right behind us – within the walls of Canna House. If you're visiting, it is a lovely space to wander about amongst the apples that you may have for dessert later that evening. There are a wide variety on offer – and we have probably made this tatin with most, so are fairly confident it will work with any apple. If you're buying apples for this dish, then a crisp, crunchy red one – a royal gala, perhaps – is the ideal choice.

In the restaurant, we serve it with a dollop of vanilla ice cream (if you're buying some, we love Mackie's).

———————

First, prepare the apples. Peel and halve them, then, by carefully cutting a shallow V-shaped valley, core them.

Cream the sugar and butter until pale and smooth.

In a roasting tin about the right size to fit the apple halves snuggly, slather the open side of each with some creamed butter/sugar and place, cut/buttered side up, in the tin.

Once the butter/cream has been evenly distributed across all the apples, and they're all in the tin, cover with tin foil. Roast at 180°C for 3–4 hours, removing the foil for the last 30 minutes. They should have coloured nicely and be very soft, but should still retain their shape.

Whilst still warm, in each ramekin place two halves back together with the join running vertically, so that the apple is back together – you may need to squish it a bit, which is fine. If space, pour some of the melted sauce in too.

Serves 4 (1 tart each – you'll need 4 ramekins, each around 5cm in diameter)

For the tarte tatins

4 apples

150g caster sugar

150g unsalted butter

16cm sheet of puff pastry (frozen) (you'll need an 8cm square per apple)

For the caramel sauce

100g caster sugar

50g butter

200ml double cream

Once cooled, these can be stored in the fridge for a week.

Now for the caramel sauce. Add the sugar and a tiny amount of water to a small saucepan – the water shouldn't cover the sugar, just dampen it. Place on a medium-high heat and do not stir. The sugar will melt – if it is doing so unevenly, tilt or move the pan around.

Once liquid, it will eventually start to brown – you'll see a wisp of dark smoke. At this point add the butter (with caution). It will bubble dramatically, but mix it in.

Add about half of the cream – again, it will go a little crazy, but don't worry, just mix it in.

At this point, evaluate the colour (do not taste it – it will burn). Add as much cream as possible, whilst not letting it become too light. You want a rich brown caramel.

To serve, place each of the apple ramekins on a baking tray with an approximately 8cm square of thin (3–4mm) puff pastry sitting on top, well centred.

Place in an oven preheated to 210°C for 12 minutes, or until the puff pastry is cooked and crisp.

To plate – and take care with this – take a still warm/hot ramekin and, making sure you protect your hand from scalding (e.g. with a clean dish towel), turn it upside down so that the pastry sits on the plate with the apple above. Remove the ramekin, drizzle some caramel sauce on top and add a scoop of ice cream.

Cranachan baked alaska

Famously difficult to serve, baked alaska is as 1980s as it is show-off chef. The thing is, you need to bake meringue around ice cream, without melting the ice cream. It first went through our kitchen in response to a challenge, and it went surprisingly well.

Putting it on the menu meant it needed to be do-able, but also easy to serve in the heat of a service, so we came up with this variation. It allows individual alaskas to be stored frozen, with the meringue in place. To serve, all you have to do is remove it from the freezer and bake, then lap up the adoration!

Cranachan is a ubiquitous Scottish dessert of whisky, oats, cream and raspberry – we decided to make an ice-cream version of this and have that as the centre of the alaska.

———

First, make the cranachan ice cream.

Combine the honey, oil and salt in a pan and heat gently, then add the oats. Spread this mixture thinly on to a baking tray and bake at 170°C for 20 minutes. Remove and cool.

Push the raspberries through a sieve or use a juicer to extract their juice. Stir in the icing sugar and put to one side.

Whip the cream to peaks and add the condensed milk and whisky, then whip again to soft peaks.

Fold in the crunchy oat mixture.

Churn this cranachan mix in an ice-cream machine, drizzling the raspberry juice in on the final few turns. Place in the freezer to harden up.

Serves 6–8

For the cranachan ice cream

3 tbsp honey

1½ tbsp sunflower oil

a pinch of salt

100g oats

300g raspberries

2 tbsp icing sugar

600ml double cream

350g condensed milk

50ml whisky

For the sponge base

1 egg

2 tbsp sugar

3 tbsp plain flour

½ teaspoon baking powder

¼ teaspoon cornflour

2 tbsp unsalted butter

2 tbsp milk

For the meringue

120g egg white

200g caster sugar

For the sponge base, beat the egg and sugar together to the consistency of whipped cream. Add and gently fold in the flour, baking powder and cornflour. Melt the butter and combine with the milk, then fold into the mix.

Line a tray with greaseproof paper. Pour the mixture onto the tray to approximately 1cm thickness, then bake at 180°C for 10–12 minutes. Let it cool, then transfer to a wire rack.

For the meringue, in a large bowl whisk the egg whites and sugar. Once soft peaks have been achieved, sit the bowl on a pan with an inch or so of water simmering away in it and continue to whisk until the sugar has melted (use your fingertips to see if it feels grainy). Once all the sugar has disappeared, remove the bowl from the pan and whisk until cool. It should be thick and airy.

To construct the dessert, cut circles in the desired size out of the sponge base – it's useful to base these on, for example, a small mug (see the next step).

Line a small mug with cling film and press some of the ice cream into it firmly to mould it into shape. Remove from the mug/cling film and position on top of the sponge base.

Spoon meringue onto and around the ice cream so that is it completely and thickly surrounded, then place in the freezer.

Preheat the oven to 200°C. Take the alaskas from the freezer and place on a baking tray. Bake for 10 minutes. Serve immediately

Consider adding some more whisky to the bowls and setting alight for added drama!

Sea buckthorn sorbet

Sea buckthorn is a fabulous ingredient, with tart, juicy berries and another horribly spiky bush to pick them from! Whilst not naturally found on Canna, this shrub is prevalent across much of Scotland – particularly on the east coast. As on most of the Western Isles, it does grow in pockets, though (such as in our garden!).

To harvest and process the berries, it is a case of collecting them at the right time in the season (late summer), when they are plump and orange but not so ripe that they turn to mush on contact. You can extract the juice using a potato ricer.

The sorbet has a sweet sourness unlike any other. It goes extremely well with a rich dessert. We serve it with a dark chocolate torte.

———————

Pour the water, glucose syrup (if using) and sugar into a small saucepan and bring to the boil. Reduce the heat and simmer for 5 minutes to make a syrup. Leave to cool before continuing.

Mix in the sea buckthorn juice and churn the mixture in an ice-cream machine or, if you don't have one, place in the freezer and stir every 30 minutes until you can't stir any longer.

Put in the freezer to harden a little before serving.

Makes approx. 500ml

250ml water

200g sugar

70g glucose syrup (optional, but makes the sorbet considerably less solid and icy)

500ml sea buckthorn juice

Acknowledgements

As I say elsewhere in the book, there are plenty of people that are owed a lot. I'd like to thank . . .

The community. It's an amazing thing to have a whole island of people who have got your back. It's maybe not something that you might think about when visiting, but everything on the island – the road, pier, power, paths, water, livestock – is maintained on the ground by the community. On a day-to-day basis there isn't really anybody else to call upon. Same for Café Canna. When the power goes down during service, or parts of the building float away in a storm, it's those same people who are there to help. You've all chipped in when we've needed it – and all participated enthusiastically (very enthusiastically) when there's a party to be had. Thanks to all of you, and particularly Chris, Anna and Caroline for helping me get set up way back at the start. I had no idea what I was doing – and then I slightly did. That was down to you, and I cannot be more appreciative.

Pete, our resident musician, one-man pantomime performer, ping-pong champion and so many other things it would be hard work to list them all. You deserve a special mention too. Always ready to turn an OK night into a belter and up for helping in any way at any time. Thank you, Pete!

Winnie and Liz, the oracles – the source of a lot of my inspiration and knowledge when it comes to foraging for food. I think I'd still be hunting for clams or collecting potentially hazardous plants if it weren't for you.

Simon Hird. Thanks for the incredible photos, the good laugh, for staying longer than you needed to and then mucking in like a champ when you did.

The National Trust for Scotland, who own and manage Canna. It's a challenging position to be in and we're thankful for the support received.

The Calmac freight crew. Deliveries to the island are never straightforward and depend on all sorts of things. Your support and sarcasm are ever-important to us.

My dad. I'm pretty certain the retirement plan didn't include kp duties or baking, accountancy, painting or becoming the suavest meeter-and-greeter in the land, but your support was there from the start and has never waned.

Guy, fixer of things and one-man bottling machine, and my mum. Thanks so much for absolutely everything.

Fiona. If you've dined or had a drink with us, it's likely that you've had the pleasure of using some of the stunning pottery that we all try so very hard not to break – but often do. All made by hand and every piece a work of art.

Bella Jane/AquaXplore boat trips. Canna is visited many times daily by boats based off the neighbouring Isle of Skye. It's a fantastic experience and allows Canna and its wildlife to be appreciated from the sea – one of the best ways going. They're as keen as we are on the place and this shines through in the faces of the visitors they bring to Canna.

Finally, it goes without saying – to all our incredible customers. An interest in the island, its produce and what we're doing with it was where this book began. We love being here, and love doing this, and so thanks beyond measure for coming along for the ride.

Index